Walking Roman Roads in East Cumbria

by Philip Graystone S.M.

with an introductory essay
by David Shotter

Centre for North-West Regional Studies
University of Lancaster
1994

General Editor, Oliver M. Westall

Walking Roman Roads in East Cumbria
by Philip Graystone,
with an introductory essay by David Shotter

This volume is the twenty-ninth in a series published by the Centre for North-West Regional Studies at the University of Lancaster. Details of other titles in the series which are available may be found at the back of this volume.

ISSN 0308–4310

Published by the Centre for North-West Regional Studies,
University of Lancaster, 1994

Typeset in Linotype Stempel Garamond by Carnegie Publishing Ltd,
18 Maynard St, Preston, Lancs.
Printed at Alden Press Limited,
Oxford and Northampton, Great Britain

British Library Cataloguing in Publication Data
A CIP record for this book is available from the British Library

ISBN 0-901800-34-1

Preface

THIS account of the Maiden Way and the Stanegate is the second volume in the series describing the principal Roman roads in the North-West. Like the first, it is intended for the outdoor enthusiast, but every effort has been made to ensure archaeological and historical accuracy, as the numerous references and bibliography will testify.

My grateful thanks are due to all the people who gave me permission to explore traces of Roman roads in odd corners of their farms, and indeed sometimes directed me to unsuspected localities; also very sincerely, to Barbara and Miles Sharratt, my companions along every yard of these fascinating roads.

Philip Graystone
January 1994

Contents

Introduction

THE two roads we will be following in this volume are the Maiden Way, throughout its length, from Kirkby Thore to Carvoran, and the Stanegate in its western part, from Vindolanda to Carlisle. Hence some apology for the title of the book is in order, since neither of the roads lies wholly within the county of Cumbria. But I hope readers will agree that no apology is needed for the choice of the roads themselves. Each in its distinct way (and they differ greatly) is a spectacular piece of Roman engineering, well preserved over long stretches and mostly easily accessible.

This book is intended primarily for the walker, who must be prepared for rough ground and heavy going, especially in following the Maiden Way. The maps accompanying the text are only rough sketches, intended, not for navigation, but to give some idea of the whereabouts of the various photographs. For navigation purposes the reader will need to arm him/herself with the excellent series of Ordnance Survey Pathfinder maps of this area, to which constant reference is made in the text and which are, indeed, quite indispensable for the serious student of the Roman Roads. The serial numbers of the maps required are, for the Maiden Way, 578, 569, 559, for the Stanegate, 545, and for both roads the overlapping map 546. This represents a rather formidable outlay, but one which is well worthwhile in terms of usefulness and adding to the enjoyment of the venture. The one-inch O.S. Landranger maps, 91 and 96, offer a more economical alternative, but a far less satisfactory one in information and guidance.

Notes on access are included at the end of each chapter – to a great extent both roads are either accompanied by rights of way or can be viewed from publicly accessible points; where this is not so permission should, of course, be sought.

Roads, Maps and Place-Names

David Shotter

THE continuing fascination of Roman Roads lies largely in the fact
that so many stretches of them can still be detected in town and
country, and that they therefore remain a tangible link with a period
of our history that has always evoked striking images. A parallel
interest, of course, lies in the study of the places which are linked by
these roads, and particularly of the names that were assigned to them.
Over the years, much has depended on varying interpretations of
three major 'map-like' documents which survive from the Roman
period: the *Antonine Itinerary*, the *Notitia Dignitatum* and the
Ravenna Cosmography.

The introduction to this, the second of Philip Graystone's *Walk-ing Roman Roads*, will explore the role of such documents in allow-ing us to reconstruct the map of the north-west of Roman Britain.

A number of preliminary points need to be made; first, the
documents in question appear to apply to different periods and have
different purposes. We should not, therefore, be altogether surprised
if they appear to contain evidence which is inconsistent. Obviously,
however, the evidence which they provide relates to their dates of
compilation, and that evidence becomes usable if we can pin-point
such dates. Secondly, these documents do *not*, of course, exist in
their *original* forms; they have been copied, thus putting the modern
student to some degree at least at the mercy of the copyist. Distances
in figures, such as are provided in the *Antonine Itinerary*, are notor-iously vulnerable to manuscript corruption. Thirdly, we can pin-point
site-names with confidence only when they appear on inscriptions
which clearly derive from the sites.

Fourthly, since we are dealing with documents which derive from
particular periods, we can apply the information which they contain
only when we have acceptable chronological frameworks from the
sites in question. It has to be noted that this is still only rarely the
case with sites in north-west England. Finally, it is tempting to apply
sequences of names in these documents to sequences of sites on the
ground. However, caution is advisable since previously unknown
sites are still discovered through field-work and aerial photography,
and thus apparent sequences of sites on the ground may be mislead-ing; in the north-west, the recent discovery of sites such as Burgh I
and Blennerhasset in Cumbria serves to demonstrate this point. It is

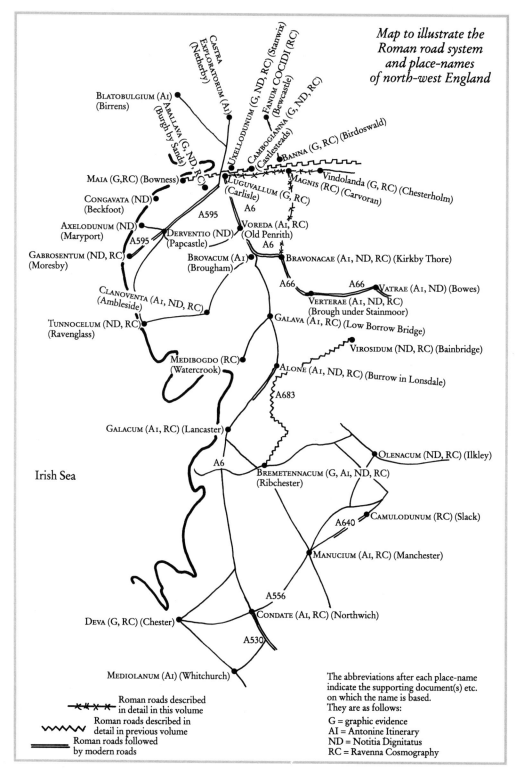

Map to illustrate the
Roman road system
and place-names
of north-west England

CASTRA
EXPLORATORIUM (AI)
(Netherby)

UXELLODUNUM (G, ND, RC) (Stanwix)

FANUM COCIDI (RC)
(Bewcastle)

BLATOBULGIUM (AI)
(Birrens)

ABALLAVA (G, ND, RC)
(Burgh by Sands)

CAMBOGIANNA (G, ND, RC)
(Castlesteads)

BANNA (G, RC) (Birdoswald)

MAIA (G,RC) (Bowness)

Vindolanda (G, RC) (Chesterholm)

MAGNIS (RC) (Carvoran)

LUGUVALLUM (G, RC)
(Carlisle)

CONGAVATA (ND)
(Beckfoot)

A6

AXELODUNUM (ND)
(Maryport)

A595

VOREDA (AI, RC)
(Old Penrith)

DERVENTIO (ND)
(Papcastle)

A595

A6

GABROSENTUM (ND, RC)
(Moresby)

BROVACUM (AI)
(Brougham)

BRAVONACAE (AI, ND, RC) (Kirkby Thore)

CLANOVENTA (AI, ND, RC)
(Ambleside)

A66

A66

VATRAE (AI, ND) (Bowes)

VERTERAE (AI, ND, RC)
(Brough under Stainmoor)

TUNNOCELUM (ND, RC)
(Ravenglass)

GALAVA (AI, RC) (Low Borrow Bridge)

VIROSIDUM (ND, RC) (Bainbridge)

MEDIBOGDO (RC)
(Watercrook)

ALONE (AI, ND, RC) (Burrow in Lonsdale)

A683

GALACUM (AI, RC) (Lancaster)

OLENACUM (ND, RC) (Ilkley)

Irish Sea

A6

BREMETENNACUM (G, AI, ND, RC)
(Ribchester)

A640

CAMULODUNUM (RC) (Slack)

MANUCIUM (AI, RC) (Manchester)

A556

DEVA (G, RC) (Chester)

CONDATE (AI, RC) (Northwich)

A530

MEDIOLANUM (AI) (Whitchurch)

The abbreviations after each place-name
indicate the supporting document(s) etc.
on which the name is based.
They are as follows:

✕✕✕✕ Roman roads described
in detail in this volume

〜〜〜 Roman roads described in
detail in previous volume

Roman roads followed
by modern roads

G = graphic evidence
AI = Antonine Itinerary
ND = Notitia Dignitatus
RC = Ravenna Cosmography

also worth pointing out that often, when identifications of sites and place-names have been made (on whatever evidence), they prove to be notoriously resistant to argument and time. An example is the association of MEDIBOGDO of the *Ravenna Cosmography* with the fort at Hardknott Pass. Nor should we assume necessarily that known place-names are unique to a single site.

I. *Sites and inscriptions*

Few Roman sites in north-west England can with confidence be assigned names on the evidence of inscriptions, although the identifications of DEVA with Chester, of BREMETENNACUM with Ribchester, and of LUGUVALLIUM with Carlisle all seem certain and acceptable.[1] Further, objects such as the Rudge Cup and Amiens *patera*[2] provide sequences of sites on Hadrian's Wall, making it reasonably certain that we can accept:

MAIA	Bowness-on-Solway
ABALLAVA	Burgh-by-Sands
PETRIANA/UXELLODUNUM	Stanwix
CAMBOGLANNA	Castlesteads
BANNA	Birdoswald

We should notice here that there appears to be no acceptable name for Drumburgh, that there appear to be two names in use for Stanwix, one of which derives from the unit in garrison (*Ala Petriana*) and that the association of BANNA with Birdoswald appears to be confirmed by an inscription referring to *Venatores Banniesses* (huntsmen from BANNA).[3]

Although these identifications represent only a very small proportion of Roman sites in north-west England, their value is enhanced by the fact that versions of the same names appear in other documents, thus providing a basis for further suggestions. Similarly, 'cross referencing' may be possible at those sites at which inscriptions specify the presence of particular garrison-units, which are also mentioned in the *Notitia Dignitatum*. Care, however, needs to be exercised here, since units were moved around, and in that case 'cross-referencing' can be attempted only if we are confident of the chronological propriety in particular instances.

As indicated already, a great deal depends on our ability to provide acceptable chronological frameworks for sites. Dated (or datable) inscriptions will indicate at least points at which sites were

---

[1] *Ephemeris Epigraphica* IX.1274 a and b (Chester); *RIB* 583 (Ribchester); Bowman and Thomas, 1983, Doc 22 (Carlisle).
[2] Heurgon, 1951, (Amiens Patera); Richmond, 1935 (The Rudge Cup).
[3] *RIB* 1905.

occupied, and references on inscriptions to buildings which had 'collapsed through old age' *may* indicate the ending of a period of demilitarisation – that is, unless such references are euphemisms for more sinister activities. However, full chronological frameworks for sites can be achieved only as a result of substantial programmes of excavation, and there are still very many sites in north-west England that have seen no excavation at all or at best only 'trial trenches'. Even when substantial excavations have taken place we have to be cautious before assuming that the parts of the site that have been tested are necessarily chronologically typical of the *whole* site. Thus, excavations such as those at Watercrook in 1974 and 1975 which were concerned primarily with areas which were extra-mural to the fort may not provide a reliable picture of the chronology of *military* occupation at the site.

II. *The Antonine Itinerary*[4]

This is a document of the first quarter of the third century AD, which derives its name from the assumption of the name, Antoninus, by rulers of the Severan dynasty. In this case, the reference is probably to Septimius Severus' elder son, Caracalla, who reigned as emperor between AD 211 and 217.

This 'work' has come down to us in the form of 'routes', consisting of lists of place-names with distances between them. Routes II, V and X are concerned with journeys which lie in whole or part in north-west England; whilst II and V cross respectively out of and into north-west England apparently by way of Stainmore, X is wholly within the region. It is a route of 150 miles from CLANO-VENTA, via GALAVA, ALONE, GALACVM, BREMETONNACUM COCCIUM, MAMVCIVM, and CONDATE, to MEDIOLANVM. It has to be said that there is no supporting evidence for most of the traditional place-name identifications on the route – from Ravenglass, via Ambleside, Watercrook, Burrow-in-Lonsdale, Ribchester, Wigan, Manchester, and Northwich, to Whitchurch. As we have seen, only Ribchester can be supported as BREMETONNACUM. Unfortunately, such inscribed milestones as survive offer no clues to identifications; only that found at Caton (*RIB* 2272) appears to contain a vestigial name, presumably of Lancaster, but it cannot be interpreted.

As far as occupation-patterns are concerned, we know little of Burrow-in-Lonsdale and Wigan, whilst there is a likelihood that neither Watercrook nor Northwich saw occupation at the relevant time. In any case, the identification of ALONE (Alauna) with a site on the river Kent does not seem appropriate. A clue may be provided by a dedication found at Bolton-le-Sands to the god, Ialonus (*RIB*

---

4 Rivet, 1970.

600); the discovery of this unique deity in the area of the Lune valley prompts the suggestion that he might have been the river's presiding spirit. On etymological grounds, it might then be reasonable to assign GALAVA, ALONE and GALACVM to Lune Valley sites – presumably respectively Low Borrow Bridge, Burrow-in-Lonsdale and Lancaster. This would render it impossible to continue to identify CLANOVENTA with Ravenglass. In any case, the name (which means 'market by the clear water') could apply to any site with an aquatic connection; in this case, a possible candidate is Brougham, which by its position was probably an important market-centre, though this identification would create interpretative problems with routes II and V. A better identification for CLANOVENTA is Ambleside; the name aptly suits the position of the site, and recent work at Ambleside[5] has suggested that the civilian-settlement outside the fort may have been quite extensive.

South of Ribchester, COCCIVM might be Wigan; although the Roman origin of that town is now beyond doubt, little is known of its nature or chronology, and some continue to prefer to 'reserve' the name for a site still to be located – perhaps in the region of Affetside. That MAMVCIVM should be identified with Manchester appears reasonable, from where Northwich (CONDATE) and Whitchurch (MEDIOLANVM) would not appear to be unreasonable destinations. Little of this, however, can be argued further without the discovery of fresh epigraphic evidence.

Routes II and V of the *Antonine Itinerary* are apparently concerned with the north of the region, since they involve both York and Carlisle, and thus evidently a crossing of the Pennines by way of the Stainmore Pass. Route II starts at BLATOBULGIUM and proceeds to CASTRA EXPLORATORUM (*Fort of the Scouts*) and LVGVVALLVM. Since there can be little doubt that the latter is Carlisle, the suggestions that the first two are Birrens and Netherby seem wellfounded. South of Carlisle, the route runs through VOREDA, BROVONACAE, VERTERAE and LAVATRAE to CATARACTONE, ISVRIVM and EBVRACVM. The last three are to be identified with Catterick, Aldborough and, of course, York. The stated distances of stages between Carlisle and Catterick are consistent with identifying VOREDA with Old Penrith, BROVONACAE with Kirkby Thore, VERTERAE with Brough-under-Stainmore and LAVATRAE with Bowes. Such chronological information as we currently possess is consistent with postulating occupation at all of these sites at the time relevant to the *Antonine Itinerary* – that is, the first quarter of the third century AD.

Route V is concerned with a journey northwards from London to Carlisle (LVGVVALIVM), and towards the end has a sequence of EBVRACVM, ISVBRIGANTVM, CATARACTONE, LAVATRAE and VERTERAE;

---

[5] For a summary of recent work, see CW[2] XCIII (1983), 51–74

this is the same sequence, though, of course, in reverse order, that appears in route II. There is, however, in route V no mention after VERTERAE of BROVONACAE and VOREDA. Instead, the only site mentioned between VERTERAE (Brough-under-Stainmore) and LVGVVALIVM (Carlisle) is BROCAVVM. Whilst this could conceivably represent a manuscript-corruption (involving BROVONACAE), it seems more likely that BROCAVVM is to be identified with Brougham which, as we have seen, stood, like its medieval counterpart, at a significant road-junction. There is no obvious explanation for this divergence between routes II and V.

From the Antonine Itinerary, therefore, we can postulate the names of some sixteen Roman sites and their modern counterparts in north-west England.

III. *The Notitia Dignitatum*[6]

The *Notitia Dignitatum*, which has long generated much discussion, appears to comprise a complete or near-complete list of military commanders, their armies and dispositions in the late empire. The document, however, raises a number of complex and far-reaching problems. It appears to represent an official compilation, though it is in this case surprising that the information contained in it does not appear to conform to a single period of compilation. The possibility, therefore, remains that the *Notitia may* represent an unofficial compilation by persons unknown.[7]

The dating and purpose of the *Notitia* have been subjects of much speculation, as have the identities of site-names and military units listed in the section referring to the command of the officer known as the *Dux Britannarium* (Duke of the Britains), who was based at York and controlled the northern frontier-area. It is generally held that most of the information relating to Britain belongs to the second half of the fourth century, although that contained in the 'wall sub-section'[8] *may* date from the previous century. This suggestion has been made because, whilst the bulk of the military units listed in the Duke's command consist of 'irregulars', most of whom are not instanced elsewhere, those in the 'wall sub-section' are *cohortes* and *alae* known to have been in Britain, and often at the forts in question, during the third century. On the other hand, it should be noted that increasingly excavation at Hadrian's Wall forts is suggesting that some at least were unoccupied or barely occupied in the second half of the third century.

Further, considerable problems are caused by the fact that, with

---

[6] Goodburn and Bartholomew, 1976.
[7] Stevens, 1950.
[8] Gillam, 1949.

the exception of the 'wall sub-section', the sites are listed not in apparent conformity with any geographical or military logic – unless, of course, this is lost because of our general ignorance of place-name identification in northern Britain. Again, there is some evidence of textual disturbance in the portion dealing with the western end of Hadrian's Wall.[9]

The 'wall sub-section' contains some names familiar from the Rudge Cup, although the textual disturbance, referred to above, causes some problems of interpretation. It is reasonable to suppose that the western sequence includes Castlesteads (AMBOGLANNA) and Stanwix (UXELLODUNUM/PETRIANAE); however, the name (though *not* the military unit) of Birdoswald has been lost, and this has led to the long-standing misidentification of that site as CAMBOGLANNA. Burgh-by-Sands appears as ABALLABA, but there is no apparent listing of Drumburgh or Bowness-on-Solway, although we know from excavation that Bowness at least was occupied in the second half of the fourth century.

Beyond ABALLABA, the names CONGAVATA, AXELODUNUM, GABRO-SENTUM, TUNNOCELUM and GLANNIBANTA have been taken to be forts on the Cumberland coast – Beckfoot, Maryport, Burrow Walls, Moresby and Ravenglass. Of the military units given in the *Notitia*-list, some are known from epigraphic evidence to have been garrisoned at coastal sites. For instance, *Cohors* I Hispanorum is known at Maryport, whilst *Cohors* II Lingonum and *Cohors* II Thracum are both evidenced at Moresby. Further, a lead sealing of *Cohors* I Aelia Classica was found in excavations at Ravenglass in the late 1970s.[10]

It is possible in view of this that we could postulate identifications of CONGAVATA/Beckfoot, AXELODUNUM/Maryport, GABROSENTUM/Moresby, and TUNNOCELUM/Ravenglass. GLANNIBANTA could then be identified with Ambleside (CLANOVENTA of the *Antonine Itinerary*). The apparent omission of Hardknott does not cause problems since the dating-evidence for the site suggests that it was not occupied in the fourth century. There is then no reason why ALIONE should not be Burrow-in-Lonsdale, particularly since the next site to be listed is BREMETENRACUM/Ribchester.

The Duke's list in the *Notitia* also includes LAVATRAE, VERTERAE, and BRABONIACUM; this sequence appears to preserve that in the *Antonine Itinerary*, which has been identified as belonging to the Stainmore route – Bowes, Brough and Kirkby Thore. Moreover, the unit placed at VERTERAE, the *numerus directorum* (or unit of dispatches), would be appropriate for Brough, a site which has produced such a large and variable collection of lead-sealings for official

[9] Hassall, 1976.
[10] Shotter, 1979, 73f.

packages.[11] MAGLONE and MAGIS are placed after BRABONIACUM and, as we have seen, there is reason to suppose that one of these *might* be Old Carlisle.

This leaves unidentified MAGIS (or MAGLONE), LONGOVICIUM (which appears at this point but *may* be a site in the north-east), DERVENTIO (often taken as Papcastle, which in view of its probable significance would be expected to have had a place in the list), and finally OLENACUM and VIROSIDUM (which *could* be Ilkley and Bainbridge). These postulated identifications do not restore total logic to the list in *Notitia*, or solve all of the problems, but they do provide *some* geographical connections and sequences.

iv. *The Ravenna Cosmography*[12]

This document of the seventh century appears to derive in part from a road-map; lists of names radiate from centres which are mentioned once and subsequently have to be understood at the commencement of each route for which they are the starting-point – a feature which is bound in view of the general paucity of our knowledge to occasion confusion. As we attempt to make sense of the Ravenna-listings, we must again bear in mind the need for caution in view of the fact that many of the site-identifications postulated above, and which are employed in this section, have to be treated as tentative.

A start may be made with MAUTIO, which should evidently be identified with Manchester; this is apparently the starting-point for four routes – to ALICUNA (Ilkley), to CAMULODUNUM (Slack?), and to CALUVIO (Lancaster), whilst the fourth runs to BRESMETENACUM VET-ERANORUM (Ribchester) into west Yorkshire. It should be noticed that place-names are not necessarily listed on *every* route on which they feature. Thus, Ribchester is listed on the route which heads from Manchester into west Yorkshire, but *not* on that to Lancaster.

Within the list of routes leading from Manchester, there appear to be subsidiary 'departure-points', thus, after CALUVIO (Lancaster) come GALLUVIO (Low Borrow Bridge), MEDIBOGDO, CANTIVENTI, IULIOCENON and GABROCENTIO. Of these, MEDIBOGDO ('fort in the middle of a bow') would appear to provide a fitting description of the fort and *vicus* at Watercrook, situated as they are in a deep loop of the River Kent. If so, this seems to represent a fresh departure from Lancaster, leading to Ambleside (if CANTIVENTI is to be identified with CLANOVENTA of the *Antonine Itinerary*), and then to Ravenglass (assuming that IULIOCENON is the TUNNOCELUM of the *Notitia Dignitatum*), and Moresby (GABROCENTIO/GABROSENTUM).

---

[11] Richmond, 1936.
[12] Richmond and Crawford, 1949.

ALAUNA, which follows GABROCENTIO, has usually been identified with Maryport, but might in fact represent a further departure from Lancaster along the Lune valley, heading for Burrow-in-Lonsdale.

It has to be said that this leaves us with difficulties over the identification of BRIBRA, MAIO, OLERICA, DERVENTIO, and RAVONIA. BRIBRA might be identified with VIROSIDUM of the *Notitia* as Bainbridge, from which two routes conceivably lead – one into Yorkshire (to DERVENTIO/Malton), the other to RAVONIA, which has often been taken as BRABONIACUM, or Kirkby Thore.

Kirkby Thore then becomes a new departure point: first, a route leads to VALTERIS (probably Brough-under-Stainmore), and then a second to BEREDA (Old Penrith) and LAGUBALIUM (Carlisle). A third leads apparently along the Maiden Way to a new centre – MAGNIS, which is probably to be identified with Carvoran, a fort occupying a position both on Hadrian's Wall, and on its predecessor, the Stanegate. Although the Stanegate enjoyed a significant role as a traditional frontier (*limes*) in the late first and early second centuries, its official importance must have diminished to a certain extent after the placing of forts along Hadrian's Wall, and the construction of the Military Way. Yet it linked sites whose importance continued – Carlisle, Corbridge, and, of course, Chesterholm (VINDOLANDA), which actually figures as a site in the 'wall sub-section' of the *Notitia*. Indeed, it is to VINDOLANDA that one route from Carvoran leads in the Ravenna-listing.

The approach to Carvoran along the Maiden Way also reflects a route of importance, since it linked Stainmore with Hadrian's Wall, passing the heavily-defended Pennine fort of Whitley Castle. This fort probably enjoyed a significance which stemmed from the job of its garrison in protecting the development of the lead/silver industry in the area. Not only was the silver important for coinage, but the lead too must have been in heavy demand for use in construction. The significance of the link between Stainmore and Hadrian's Wall is highlighted by the role which, on the basis of the evidence of the finds of lead-sealings and the name of the garrison assigned to it in the *Notitia*, was exercised by the fort at Brough-under-Stainmore.

Another departure from MAGNIS – this time along the Military Way – was to GABAGLANDA, which, as we have seen, was probably the Hadrian's Wall fort of Castlesteads. A new starting point is then picked out on this route – BANNA (Birdoswald); from here a route follows the Military Way, taking in UXELLODUNUM (probably Stanwix), AVALAVA (Burgh-by-Sands), and MAIA (Bowness-on-Solway). A second route from BANNA leads to FANUM COCIDI, which on the evidence there for the god, Cocidius (or Mars Cocidius), was probably Bewcastle.[13]

---

13 Birley, 1961, 233.

Further south, the *Cosmography's* listing gives a clear sequence of DEVA VICTRIX (Chester) and CONDATE (Northwich).

Although much remains unclear, this short discussion indicates that there is room for re-arrangement of routes long thought to be fixed and for a re-thinking of traditionally-accepted site-identifications. Fresh certainty, however, can be achieved only with the discovery of new inscriptions which can provide us with unequivocal identifications.

Finally, a word should be said about the site of PORTUS SETANTIORUM which figures in the *Geographia* of Ptolemy of Alexandria who made his compilation in the mid-second century AD. It is usually assumed that this is a site which has been lost through coastal change, and now lies off Fleetwood beneath the waters of the Lune estuary. Some weight is added to this idea by the fact that a road from Ribchester leads westward through the Fylde to Kirkham, and then onwards as if making for the mouth of the river Wyre, where a considerable amount of Roman material has been found over the years.

It is, of course, a story which readily lends itself to romantic embroidery. We should, however, bear in mind that a recent discussion[14] has suggested the placing of the Setantii in southern Cumbria, an area where a number of significant hill-forts possibly points to the existence of a tribal group (or sub-group) of some importance. An accumulating body of circumstantial evidence points to the likelihood of the use of Windermere as an alternative to road-transport for conveying men and materials into the heart of the Lake District. If there was a fort at the southern end of the lake, with a responsibility for the dispatch of such cargoes, it might not be thought inappropriate if its name was PORTUS SETANTIORUM.

References

Arch. Ael   *Archaeologia Aeliana*

CW²   Transactions of the Cumberland and Westmorland Antiquarian and Archaeological Society

JRS   Journal of Roman Studies

RIB   Roman Inscriptions of Britain

Birley, 1961: Birley, E. B., *Research on Hadrian's Wall*, Kendal.

Bowman and Thomas, 1983: Bowman, A. K. and Thomas J. D., *Vindolanda: the Latin Writing Tablets*, London (Britannia Monographs, No. 4).

---

[14] Higham, 1986, 147. (I discuss the matter further in an article to be published in CW² XCIV (1994).)

Gillam, 1949: Gillam J. P., Also, 'Along the Line of the Wall', *CW*² XLIX, 38–58.

Goodburn and Bartholomew, 1979: Goodburn R. and Bartholomew P., *Aspects of the Notitia Dignitatum*, Oxford (British Archaeological Reports No. 15).

Hassall, 1976: Hassall M. W. C., 'Britain in the Notitia', pp. 103–17 in Goodburn and Bartholomew, 1976.

Heurgon, 1951: Heurgon J., 'The Amiens Patera', JRS XLI, 22–4.

Higham, 1986: Higham N. J., *The Northern Counties to AD 1000*, London.

Richmond, 1935: Richmond I. A., 'The Rudge Cup, II, The Inscription', *Arch. Ael.*⁴ XII, 334–42.

Richmond, 1936: Richmond I. A., 'Roman Leaden Sealings from Brough-under-Stainmore', *CW*² XXXVI, 104–25.

Richmond and Crawford, 1949: Richmond I. A. and Crawford O. G. S., 'The British Section of the Ravenna Cosmography', *Archaeologia* XCIII, 1–50.

Rivet, 1970: Rivet A. L. F., 'The British Section of the Antonine Itinerary', *Britannia J.*, 34–82.

Shotter, 1979: Shotter D. C. A., 'The Lead Sealing', pp. 73–4 in Potter T. W., *Romans in North-West England*, Kendal.

Stevens, 1950: Stevens C. E., 'A Roman Author in North-West Britain', *CW*² L, 70–9.

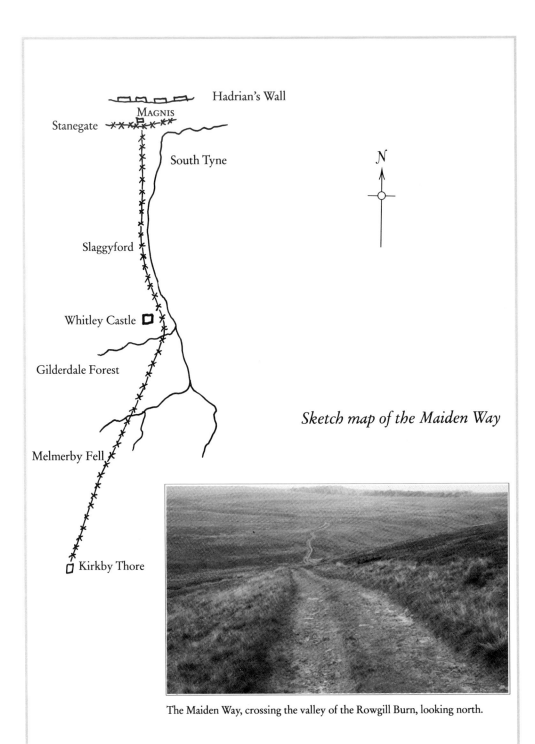

Hadrian's Wall

MAGNIS

Stanegate

South Tyne

Slaggyford

Whitley Castle

Gilderdale Forest

Melmerby Fell

Kirkby Thore

N

Sketch map of the Maiden Way

The Maiden Way, crossing the valley of the Rowgill Burn, looking north.

Part One

The Maiden Way

Chapter One

General

THE Maiden Way runs from Kirkby Thore (BRAVONIACUM) in the south to Carvoran (MAGNIS) in the north, a distance of nearly thirty miles. A little over halfway along its route (moving from south to north) is the intervening station of Whitley Castle. Like other notable Roman roads (Watling Street, Ermine Street, Dere Street and others) it is distinguished by a special name – not Roman, of course, though ancient – for which no convincing explanation has so far been offered. It is a road of quite exceptional interest. Some sections are remarkably well preserved, especially in the southern part of its course, where it climbs to a height of 2130 feet (650 metres) in crossing Melmerby Fell. As an example of Roman engineering skill it can have few equals in Britain, and being practically free of modern main roads, but frequently followed by tracks with right of access, it can for the most part be traversed on foot.

The course of the Maiden Way has been identified throughout its length, even where traces are nowadays difficult to find. Besides linking three major forts, it is thought to have another important and interesting purpose. Throughout recorded history the lead deposits around Alston have been exploited and old mine workings are frequent in the area. The Romans were probably the first in this particular field; one of the principal reasons for their invasion of Britain was its reputation as a source of metals. The Maiden Way was probably intended both to give access to the lead mines and to transport the ore away for smelting. Whitley Castle, with its elaborate defences, may well have housed soldiers supervising the mines, very likely worked by slaves and prisoners. (Higham and Jones, 1985)

A detailed survey of this road was made in 1851 by William Bainbridge (see bibliography); from time to time this will be referred to in the text, but I must confess that I have found it of limited use.

For one thing, local features which he mentions – roads, fields, boundaries, etc. – have often changed greatly since his day, and the local place names which he uses are also sometimes difficult to place precisely; for another, he persists in referring to 'right' or 'left' rather than to east, west, etc., and this can cause great confusion. In some instances I have been bold enough to disagree with Bainbridge's conclusions, even when these have been clear.

Chapter Two

From Kirkby Thore to Ardale Beck

THERE IS SOME divergence of opinion about the starting point of the Maiden Way at its southern end. Margary sees the road as branching from the great Roman highway over Stainmoor – the predecessor of the modern A66 – just south-east of the farm called Street House, almost due west of the site of the Roman fort of Kirkby Thore (BRAVONIACUM). He considers (though without giving evidence) that its course is marked by the modern minor road which leads off at this point and heads north-east for about one fifth of a mile. If this is true, then the Maiden Way would have bypassed the fort and presumably would be connected to it by a linking road. Other more recent studies, however, consider the Maiden Way as starting directly from one of the gates of Kirkby Thore, which would then of course itself be connected with the Stainmoor road. (Gibbon and others, 1989)

The present road into Kirkby Thore from the A66 runs through the site of the Roman fort, part of which is now an open field to the north of the road. Nothing now remains above ground. The site, though level, is situated on a hill-top with good views in all directions.

Bainbridge notes the first traces of the Maiden Way (working north from Kirkby Thore) as appearing just north of Hale Grange, about a mile due north of the fort. Before commenting on this, it is worth pointing out that for over a quarter of a mile south of Hale Grange a footpath (with right of way and accompanied by field boundaries) runs directly towards the fort (before swerving west). This might well represent the general direction of the Maiden Way in its early stages, especially if allowance is made for a possible small diversion in crossing, at Hale Grange, the rather steep little valley of Birk Sike. The Roman road is then, according to Bainbridge, followed by the fairly straight line of the present minor road from Hale Grange to Newbiggin Mill, a distance of about a mile and a half. Bainbridge makes the interesting observation that this stretch of road was in course of construction, on the Roman line, when he wrote in 1845; previously its Roman characteristics had been very visible.

The Hale Grange/Newbiggin Mill road is now very narrow, and bordered for some distance by high hedges, which tend to obscure its general straightness. North of Newbiggin Mill the Pathfinder

Ardale Beck

Bank Hall

N

Kirkland

Blencairn

The Maiden Way
from Kirkby Thore
to Ardale Beck

Milburn

Hale Grange

Roman
Fort

Street
House

Kirkby Thore

Maiden Way ✕✕✕✕✕✕

A66

track ....

The Maiden Way winding down the steep south side of the valley of Ardale Beck.

Looking south along the Maiden Way about three quarters of a mile north of Bank Hall; a wide, wet ridge.

The present road north of Hale Grange on the line of the Maiden Way; its directness is now virtually the only reminder of its Roman predecessor.

The view from the north of the Ardale valley, looking south along the section of the Maiden Way described in Chapter Two. The Roman road is clearly seen climbing the steep south side of the valley of Ardale Beck, and then, less distinctly, making its way over the pasture towards Bank Hall Farm. A short distance south of the Ardale valley one can just make out a semi-circular diversion in the line of the Maiden Way; this is very evident on the ground, and seems to have been caused by a building, e.g. a sheepfold, erected later when the road was still in use as a farm track. In the foreground the Maiden Way uses the deep gorge of Lad Slack to commence its climb up Melmerby Fell, as will be described in Chapter Three.

O.S. map (No. 578) shows the Maiden Way as continuing due north across the fields but there is now no trace, except perhaps for a few yards north of Underwood Farm, where a fence follows the line. The country hereabouts is, of course, farmland which has been cultivated for generations, but even so it is rather surprising that so little trace remains of a road which has left such evident signs in other parts of its route.

In fact not until Bank Hall Farm is passed – some two and a half miles north of Newbiggin Mill – does the Maiden Way begin to leave discernible signs of its route. To reach this point we must take the road to Blencairn and then on to Kirkland. Here we take the turning to the west, heading for Skipwith; a few yards along this road a track leads off northwards to Bank Hall Farm, and this is clearly, and conveniently, signed 'Maiden Way'. The track goes through the farm yard, where another sign points out the route. North of the farm yard, the track makes a V shaped zig-zag through quite a deep rock-cut cutting in order to traverse a gully and some very uneven ground. Whether this is on the Roman line is doubtful; it does not appear to figure in Bainbridge's description.

We then find ourselves crossing the open pasture to the north; here the course of the Maiden Way becomes evident, marked by a darker coloured growth of grass, heading north-eastward and climbing steadily. It is generally straight, though bending a little, perhaps to ease the gradient. In the second field beyond the farm the road becomes still clearer, with distinct traces of the ridge and with a great deal of metalling, especially where the surface is waterworn (though much of this may be the result of periodic repair in a stretch like this, which is evidently still in use).

About a mile north-east of Bank Hall Farm the Maiden Way reaches Ardale Beck; it is still represented by a hard green trackway, quite often raised, swerving somewhat to the east as it approaches the valley of the beck, then going through a cutting and turning to the west, and so gaining the valley floor by a well graded descent. A culvert carries it over the gully which is crossed before the main stream is reached.

(Note on access. The northern part of the fort site at Kirkby Thore can be viewed from the present road as described above. The footpath south of Hale Grange is a right of way, accessible from the Kirkby Thore/Newbiggin road. Hale Grange to Newbiggin Mill is a minor road, while the section north of Bank Hall is reached by the signposted track referred to in the text.)

Chapter Three

Ardale Beck to Meg's Cairn

THE actual point at which the Maiden Way crossed Ardale Beck must have coincided with the crossing place of the present track, or at any rate must have been very near it. However, the course of the Roman road immediately north of the beck seems to have been the subject of uncertainty. The modern track makes a 90° turn to the west and follows the stream bank for just under half a mile before turning abruptly north to rejoin the undoubted course of the Maiden Way further up the fell-side. On investigation, this is obviously a diversion westwards to give access to the lime kiln which is well preserved at the point where the track turns north. But this diversion apparently features on the Ordnance Survey Map of Roman Britain (1991 edition) as if it were an original feature of the Maiden Way itself. This misunderstanding (which apparently has misled Margary also) seems to arise from Bainbridge's account, in which he describes the Maiden Way as making its final descent to the stream from the north (he is working southward) by 'a gill or cleugh called Argill or Ardale'. I am convinced that by this he means, not the valley along which the Ardale Beck is marked as flowing in modern maps, but rather the gorge-like valley referred to as 'Lad Slack' on the Path-finder series, which descends southward from the fell to Ardale Beck (which, incidentally, he calls 'Ousby Beck' thus adding to the suspi-cion that his place-names hereabouts do not tally with those of the modern maps). Lad Slack runs almost due north and south, in line with the known course of the Maiden Way in both directions; it answers the description given by Bainbridge (he notes that the right or western side – he is facing south – is a 'soft slaty cliff' as is evident from the picture opposite). Finally Lad Slack contains distinct traces of the road, still used by farm vehicles to give access to the fell. The map and picture opposite might serve to make clearer this rather complex account.

At the head of Lad Slack a ridge appears in great strength, though not heading directly up the fell. Bainbridge notes several changes of direction in this very steep section – as one would expect, to ease the gradient. Higher up the fell the road – still discernible by the ridge, which is far more obvious on this high and uncultivated ground – straightens out and aligns both with the general direction of Lad Slack, and with the course of the road further south, now clearly visible as it climbs the steep south bank of Ardale and crosses the pasture towards Bank Hall Farm. A convenient fix on the Maiden

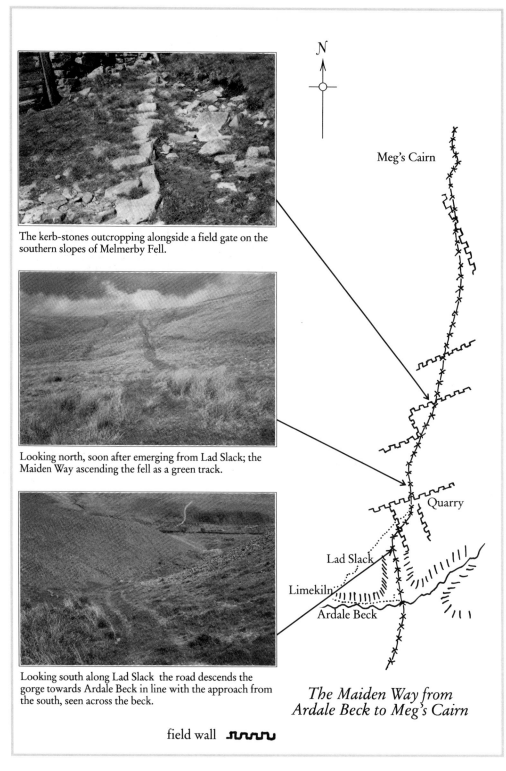

The kerb-stones outcropping alongside a field gate on the southern slopes of Melmerby Fell.

Looking north, soon after emerging from Lad Slack; the Maiden Way ascending the fell as a green track.

Looking south along Lad Slack the road descends the gorge towards Ardale Beck in line with the approach from the south, seen across the beck.

N

Meg's Cairn

Quarry

Lad Slack

Limekiln

Ardale Beck

The Maiden Way from Ardale Beck to Meg's Cairn

field wall

Way is given by the intersection of three field walls about three hundred yards north-east of the upper end of Lad Slack; from this point the road can be clearly seen climbing the fellside to the north as a green track with distinct signs of the ditches higher up the hill.

The Maiden Way then passes under the south-eastern corner of a field – conveniently marked by the right-angled intersection of bounding walls; at this point another track comes in from the south-west (it is very easy to follow this other track by mistake if one is travelling in the opposite direction – i.e. following the Roman road southward). The Maiden Way passes through a gate in the next wall, which slants across its course a short distance to the north-east; just south of this gate there is a spectacular outcrop of the kerbstones lining its eastern edge. North of the gate the road is not quite so evident; it is however making for another gate in the northern wall of the same field, and if one lines up the two gates the course becomes clear, though not altogether straight. Throughout this section of the Maiden Way, on the southern slopes of Melmerby Fell, one should be on the look-out for the occasional outcropping of the metalling, especially in wet places.

In the next rough field the Maiden Way continues as a hard grassy track, clearly marked across the field, crossing – through another gate – its eastern wall at an acute angle, and finally emerging on to the fell proper. (The succession of gates along the Maiden Way is interesting; there is little sign of its being in recent use, but it seems to have been a through route when these walls were built.) The road now enters the area of thickly scattered freestone which surrounds Meg's Cairn, a large pile some three hundred yards to the north. The Maiden Way swerves to the east to avoid the great mass of boulders immediately surrounding Meg's Cairn – certainly impenetrable now and presumably so in Roman times. Here, at the summit of the fell, is a good place for a pause in our exploration.

(Note on access. The course of the Maiden Way across Melmerby Fell – in fact from Ardale Beck to Mere Sike – is followed throughout by a footpath, which, though not shown as a right of way on Pathfinder maps, is signposted and marked by cairns and thus appears readily accessible. We shall be continuing to follow this path in the next two chapters, four and five, and for the most part it will stand out very distinctly.)

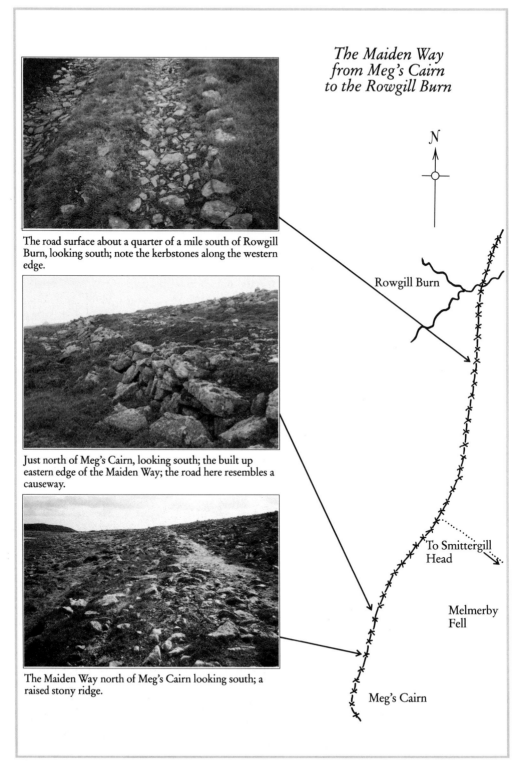

The Maiden Way from Meg's Cairn to the Rowgill Burn

N

The road surface about a quarter of a mile south of Rowgill Burn, looking south; note the kerbstones along the western edge.

Rowgill Burn

Just north of Meg's Cairn, looking south; the built up eastern edge of the Maiden Way; the road here resembles a causeway.

To Smittergill Head

Melmerby Fell

The Maiden Way north of Meg's Cairn looking south; a raised stony ridge.

Meg's Cairn

Chapter Four

Meg's Cairn to Rowgill Burn

NORTH OF MEG'S CAIRN the road enters its most spectacular section – over 2,000 feet above sea level, crossing rough moorland; it is virtually undisturbed by man, and built so strongly as to withstand the natural wear and tear of wind and rain, frost and snow. It runs straight and massive, with its edges clearly defined; in fact they are often very strongly built up with stone for considerable lengths. Building a road in this bleak and inhospitable terrain must have often been a difficult and thankless task, but at least the material lay ready to hand in abundance, and the Romans made full use of it; the road hereabouts resembles a massive stone causeway, three to four feet high. As Margary has pointed out, it is frequently in upland areas that Roman roads appear most impressively raised. Perhaps it is simply a question of survival in country never cultivated.

Also in this area the definite edging – such a feature of this road – appears at its most striking, sometimes more like a retaining wall than a kerb; mostly on the eastern side but sometimes on the other. All in all this stretch of the Maiden Way, on the summit of Melmerby Fell, must be amongst the most impressive lengths of Roman road in Britain; certainly the present author, with many years experience of walking these roads, can recall nothing to equal it.

As the road emerges from the area of freestone and commences

In the photograph above we are looking north along the Maiden Way about two-thirds of a mile south of Meg's Cairn. The road here is a hard green trackway. Notice the cutting which takes the road through the ridge of rock in the middle distance and the slight diversion caused by this.

to descend the fell, it once again resumes its covering of turf, though with many patches in which the metalling is well exposed, and with its clearly defined edging continuing as a marked feature. It is much raised, about 21 feet wide, and sometimes with traces of side ditches. Northwards from the summit its course is indicated by cairns placed at frequent intervals, though these hardly seem necessary when the remains themselves are so obvious. Soon the Rowgill valley comes into view, and the Maiden Way can be clearly seen ahead, descending to the stream and climbing up its north bank.

As the road descends the northern slopes of Melmerby Fell, it takes a more north-easterly course, following the ridge midway between Agliony Beck on the west and Smittergill Burn on the east. Further down the fell the natural curve of the ridge enables the road to resume its former course. In country of this kind the Roman engineers did not attempt the rigid alignments which they laid out in easier territory; nevertheless a glance at the Pathfinder maps shows that even in crossing such a formidable obstacle as Melmerby Fell the road still takes a very direct course. In this stretch it appears as a wide grassy track, free from the clumps of tussocky grass and heather which grow in the surrounding moor and easy to follow even without the cairns marking its line about every 200/300 yards. The metalling frequently outcrops, especially where the road is crossed by water-courses (as happens often hereabouts); the kerbs are sometimes evident, and the road is generally raised, though not so markedly as in the stretches on the summit.

About a mile and a half north-east of Meg's Cairn the Maiden Way is joined by a track coming in from the east (from Smittergill Head) and from this point almost to Mere Sike, nearly two miles on, it is maintained as a rough track giving access to shooting butts.

The Maiden Way, looking south, about half a mile north of Meg's Cairn. The road here is about 21 feet wide, grassy, raised up 3/4 feet, especially on the eastern side, with kerbstones outcropping at intervals.

Though doubtless some of the metalling is recent, especially in stretches which have been repaired, it is probable that much of the stone is the original Roman foundation, laid bare both by water action and by traffic. One notes, for example, the large size of some of the boulders – two to three feet in diameter – a point which Bainbridge mentions. Moreover the kerbstones continue to outcrop, usually only on one side, for it is probable that only part of the total width of the road remains in use – the other part often shows up as a parched strip alongside. This particular length of road, descending the northern slopes of Melmerby Fell, stands out very clearly when viewed from further north on the A686 Penrith – Alston Road, for example – and in suitable conditions of light traces of the side ditches can be discerned.

The Rowgill valley is now in view ahead, and the road is clearly seen descending to Rowgill Burn and climbing the opposite side toward the long narrow wood that marks Mere Sike. It reaches the burn just above its confluence with a tributary stream, thus avoiding the necessity of two crossings. On arrival at the Rowgill Burn the walker should be prepared for a little wading; there is in fact no other way of getting across the burn, and after heavy rain it tends to be quite deep and to flow very rapidly.

(Note on access. See the note at the end of Chapter Three. As indicated above, the Rowgill Burn can be difficult in wet weather; the bed is very rocky and care is needed when wading across.)

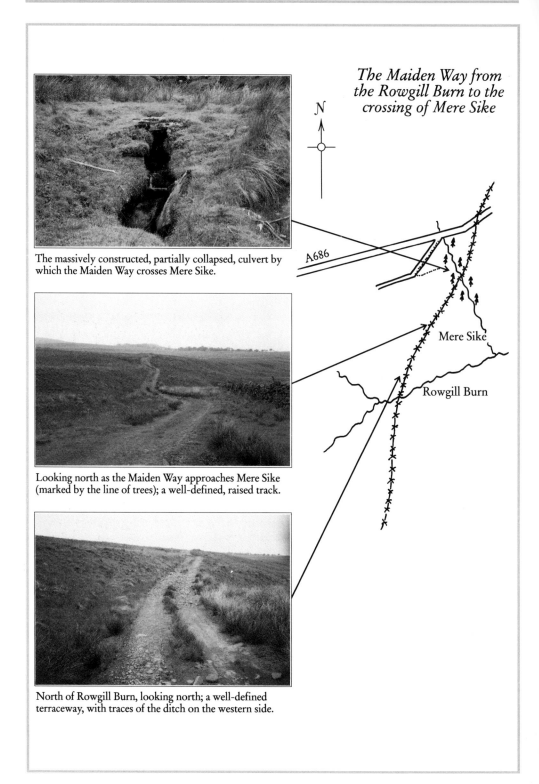

The Maiden Way from the Rowgill Burn to the crossing of Mere Sike

N

A686

Mere Sike

Rowgill Burn

The massively constructed, partially collapsed, culvert by which the Maiden Way crosses Mere Sike.

Looking north as the Maiden Way approaches Mere Sike (marked by the line of trees); a well-defined, raised track.

North of Rowgill Burn, looking north; a well-defined terraceway, with traces of the ditch on the western side.

Chapter Five

From Rowgill Burn to Mere Sike

THE modern track makes a pronounced deviation to the west to
ease the crossing of Rowgill Burn, but the O.S. Pathfinder map
shows the course of the Maiden Way maintaining its line at the
crossing, and indeed Margary points out an earth ramp on the south
bank at this point as evidence of a former bridge. The Maiden Way
continues to be well marked, and indeed still in use as a rough track,
from Rowgill Burn almost to the edge of Mere Sike. It is mostly
raised, especially on its eastern side, where outcropping kerbstones,
such a striking feature of this road, appear at intervals. Several
culverts are crossed in this section, capped by large flat stones; some
of these culverts show modern repairs, but it is worth mentioning
that Bainbridge seems to consider them Roman in origin.

Just before Mere Sike is reached from the south, the modern track
parts company with the Maiden Way and heads north and then west.
(*Sike* is evidently a dialect word for a tributary stream in these parts,
and refers to the little stream which runs almost north-south along
a wooded valley for about half a mile at this point; the wood has
been in view, as remarked above, since leaving the summit of Melmerby Fell.) Almost immediately after parting company with the
track, the Maiden Way appears to swerve to the east, possibly to
avoid a deep gully, then immediately before reaching Mere Sike from
the south-west, it appears for a short distance as a ridge between
ditches. It then descends to the stream by means of a cutting,
repeated in the north-east bank, where it is particularly wide and
distinct, making a smooth ascent in the steep bank. At the point
where the two cuttings meet, the stream is crossed by a massive
stone-built culvert, now partially collapsed, but still impressive.

Two points need to be made here. The cuttings marking the
approaches from each side, and the culvert at the same point, are a
few yards off the line of the Maiden Way as indicated on the O.S.
map. It is however well known that Roman roads frequently diverge
from their alignment as a stream is approached – to find the best
crossing point. Moreover throughout the length of Mere Sike there
is no other indication of a crossing. It can therefore be taken as
certain that this is the original Roman route. The other point is that,
given the fact that the Maiden Way is quite derelict at this point,
indeed completely overgrown by the wood bordering the Sike, both
cuttings and culvert are a fascinating survival of Roman road engineering. It is tempting to speculate that the actual construction of the

27

culvert is Roman – it certainly appears to be ancient, and even in its present ruinous state the massive capstones are very striking.

(Note on access. See note at end of Chapter Three. The track which has followed the Maiden Way across Melmerby Fell turns off just before Mere Sike is reached and heads north to link up with the A686 Penrith–Alston road.)

The Maiden Way descending the north slope of Melmerby Fell to Rowgill Burn, which is seen in the middle distance. Viewed from about 400 yards south of the A686.

Chapter Six

Mere Sike to Gilderdale Burn

A VERY USUAL FEATURE of derelict Roman roads is the alternation of well-marked stretches with lengths which have left little trace and are difficult to follow. The Maiden Way is no exception. After leaving the cutting by which it ascends the north-east bank of Mere Sike, the road immediately becomes obscure, and remains so for the next few miles. The general course is not in doubt; the road is heading for the intermediate fort of Whitley Castle, and must have maintained its north-easterly direction across Gilderdale Forest, but only occasionally can its remains be detected in this very rough, wet, and difficult country.

About half a mile after leaving Mere Sike, the Maiden Way slants across the A686 Penrith–Alston road. It then diagonally crosses two fields and for a short distance it runs immediately along – and to the west of – a wall in the third field (just to the north-west of the disused Dowhills Quarry). Here the road appears quite distinctly alongside the wall as a low, wide, grassy ridge in the surrounding rough vegetation. It remains quite derelict; indeed the fact that the next field wall crosses the line with no sign of a gate or other break indicates that it has long been so.

For the next couple of miles the Maiden Way is marked by very occasional and indefinite traces; it is evidently heading for a shallow gap in the ridge to the north-east, but not until this has been reached and passed do definite signs of the road again appear as it approaches Gilderdale Burn. Just south of the burn, at the top of the steep southern slope of the Gilderdale valley, is a wood called Wanwood Bent, through the south-western corner of which the line passes. Before this, it also passes exactly through the south-eastern angle of the second field south of Wanwood Bent, and indeed from this point the ridge is discernible running just east of north to the long narrow plantation marking the northern boundary of the same field, and from there to the point where it enters Wanwood Bent, a few yards east of the south-western corner of this rectangular wood.

Then from a point midway along the north-western boundary of the Bent, a waterworn cutting slants northwards down the valley side and appears to connect with a terrace lower down. The actual crossing point of Gilderdale Burn would appear to be about 200 yards south-west of the footbridge which carries the Pennine Way across the same burn. From this point northwards the Pennine Way

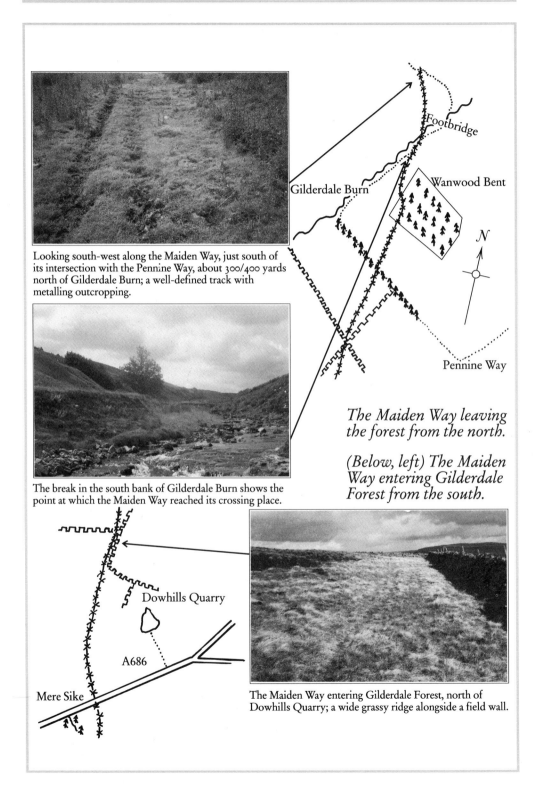

Looking south-west along the Maiden Way, just south of its intersection with the Pennine Way, about 300/400 yards north of Gilderdale Burn; a well-defined track with metalling outcropping.

Footbridge

Wanwood Bent

Gilderdale Burn

N

Pennine Way

The break in the south bank of Gilderdale Burn shows the point at which the Maiden Way reached its crossing place.

The Maiden Way leaving the forest from the north.

(Below, left) The Maiden Way entering Gilderdale Forest from the south.

Dowhills Quarry

A686

Mere Sike

The Maiden Way entering Gilderdale Forest, north of Dowhills Quarry; a wide grassy ridge alongside a field wall.

and the Maiden Way are rarely far apart, and quite often exactly coincide.

On the north side of Gilderdale Burn the Roman road climbs the very steep valley side by a terrace slanting from west to east, which though damaged and very overgrown by bracken, is nevertheless distinctly traceable in parts. At the top, near the point at which it crosses the Pennine Way, it becomes very distinct – a low ridge with traces of ditches and metalling. Here also it changes direction, from just east of north to just west of north. It has now entered the valley of the South Tyne, a river which flows almost due north – precisely the direction which the Roman engineers wished to follow. Consequently the Maiden Way now becomes a valley-side road for almost the whole remaining distance, generally less than a mile from the river, and sometimes considerably closer.

It is interesting to note that, for the next six or seven miles, the South Tyne valley determines the route not only of the Maiden Way but of the modern means of communication heading in the same general direction. Thus the A689 main road north from Alston accompanies the Roman line very closely, as does the railway (long disused but recently revived). The Romans may be said to have pioneered the use of river valleys as avenues of communication, especially in the mountainous north, showing great skill in combining the advantages of valley penetration with their overriding interest in directness and economy of distance. Well known examples are the use of the Ribble and Aire valleys in the cross-Pennine route from Ribchester to York, and of the valleys of the Lune and Eden for much of the main road north from Manchester to the Wall. Usually the Romans tended to avoid the actual valley floors, which would be marshy and liable to flooding, and site their roads some way up

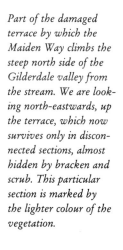

Part of the damaged terrace by which the Maiden Way climbs the steep north side of the Gilderdale valley from the stream. We are looking north-eastwards, up the terrace, which now survives only in disconnected sections, almost hidden by bracken and scrub. This particular section is marked by the lighter colour of the vegetation.

the valley side, but this is not always the case with the Maiden Way, as we shall see.

(Note on access. There is a track leading from the A686 to the disused Dowhills Quarry [though without right of way] from near which the few remaining traces in the south of Gilderdale Forest may be studied. Across the forest proper there is no public access, but this is not very important since there is so little to be seen in this area. The remains of the Maiden Way around Gilderdale Burn are mostly visible and accessible from the Pennine Way, which repeatedly crosses the Maiden Way both south and north of the burn, and is of course accompanied by right of way throughout. This section of the Pennine Way is entered from the A689 north of Sheeprigg Farm.)

Chapter Seven

Gilderdale Burn to Thornhope-burn Bridge (Lintley)

W E LEFT the Maiden Way just north of the Gilderdale valley, heading a little west of north. It is next seen, on the same line, in the field to the east of the farm marked Holymire, where the ridge appears with traces of the side ditches. Looking south along this ridge it is evident that it points directly to Wanwood Bent Wood, still clearly in view, and following the line northwards, intermittent signs of the ridge are discernible in the fields south of Castle Nook Farm, which stands upon the line.

This length of road brings us past the Roman fort of Whitley Castle; its ramparts stand out on the crest of the hill to the west of the Maiden Way, which at one point passes within a stone's throw of them, without actually entering the fort. However, for the best view of the ramparts we should make a detour so as to pass the fort on its opposite (western) side. A convenient way of doing this is to use the Pennine Way, which again crosses our route (as does the A689) at Castle Nook; if we follow it south-westwards we shall gain a fine view of the defence works.

The fort is lozenge-shaped, with its long axis set south-west to north-east. The defences are at their most spectacular along the south-western side, which is well seen from the Pennine Way about a quarter of a mile south of Castle Nook. From this point as many as eight banks and ditches stand out in bold relief. As yet no convincing explanation has been offered for such an elaborate system of defences.

Retracing our steps to Castle Nook, and crossing the A689, we find that for the next mile and a half to Lintley the Maiden Way and the Pennine Way either coincide or run close to each other. This both ensures access and acts as a handy check on our route. Actually the line is quite clear; the Maiden Way heads straight ahead, just west of north, as a ridge and hollow with a wall along its western side. The road has now entered the valley of the South Tyne and will continue roughly parallel to the river almost throughout the remainder of its length.

A short distance after leaving Castle Nook, the Maiden Way passes through another farm, Dyke House – literally in this case, for the farm buildings appear to be built on the line (and indeed to be named for the road). North of the farm a ridge and hollow continue

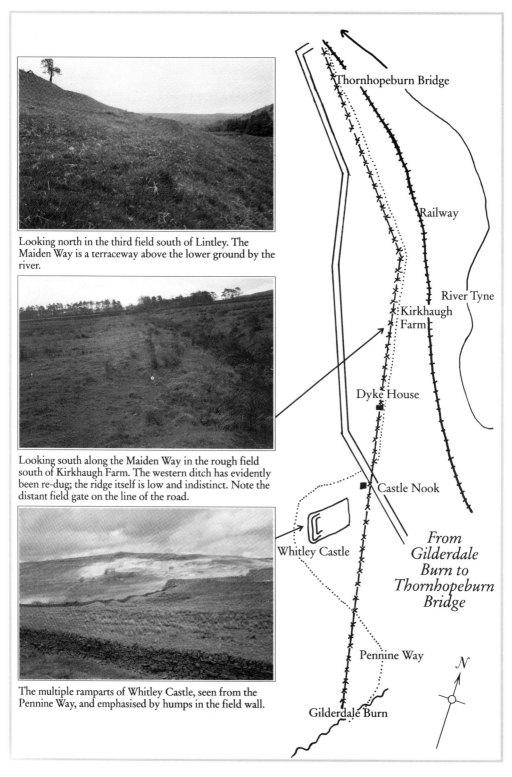

Looking north in the third field south of Lintley. The Maiden Way is a terraceway above the lower ground by the river.

Looking south along the Maiden Way in the rough field south of Kirkhaugh Farm. The western ditch has evidently been re-dug; the ridge itself is low and indistinct. Note the distant field gate on the line of the road.

The multiple ramparts of Whitley Castle, seen from the Pennine Way, and emphasised by humps in the field wall.

Thornhopeburn Bridge

Railway

River Tyne

Kirkhaugh Farm

Dyke House

Castle Nook

Whitley Castle

From Gilderdale Burn to Thornhopeburn Bridge

Pennine Way

Gilderdale Burn

N

to mark the road. The hollow, possibly marking a side ditch, runs along the west side of the low ridge, and for the first two fields the field wall continues on the western side of the hollow. It is worth noting that in this area the course of the Maiden Way is invariably marked by gates in the walls through which it passes, no doubt indicating that it was still in use, at least as a track, when these fields were enclosed.

The road now enters some quite rough pasture, where the hollow mentioned above becomes a well-marked ditch; the ridge is still discernible, the line of gates is maintained and occasionally met-alling appears. This brings the line past Kirkhaugh to the point where a slight change of direction, more to the west of north, was made by the Roman engineers. A glance at the map shows that the purpose of this was to keep the road on a course approximately parallel to the river, at this point less than half a mile away to the east. The Pennine Way bends with the Maiden Way and continues to keep close to its line until Lintley is reached, just under a mile further on; consequently stiles and gateways along the line are well maintained.

Shortly after this slight bend the Maiden Way is crossed by a modern ditch, and a line of quite heavy boulders has been exposed across the line, presumably the foundation stones of the metalling, since there are no other comparable stones in the stream bed to each side of the line. At this point there is little or no surface indication of the road, an example of how a Roman road can be substantially intact even though showing little visible trace. Further on the line does become more apparent as a green track, sometimes with slight variations in the colour of the surface vegetation and with signs of the metalling where the surface has worn away, *e.g.* at field gateways.

The Maiden Way now begins to assume the character of a terrace-way running along the first rise of land from the flood plain of the river; sometimes with signs of embankment on its lower, i.e. eastern, side. This continues across several fields, until finally the road commences to slant down to lower ground, as the crossing of the Thornhope Burn at Lintley is approached. The site of the crossing seems to be approximately marked by the footbridge which carries the Pennine Way across the burn, and a low ridge is discernible crossing the field to this point, ending in what could have been an abutment – the stream runs in a deep gorge, where a bridge would seem to be a necessity. (The situation at the burn is complicated by another, far more definite, ridge in the field to the south; this seems to indicate the course of a packhorse road mentioned by Bainbridge. Another complicating factor is the massive viaduct, only ten yards east of the footbridge, which carries the railway across Thornhope Burn.)

(Note on access. Whitley Castle is best viewed from the Pennine Way, as indicated in the text. Access to the Maiden Way on the eastern side of the fort can be gained by the farm tracks from the A689 to Whitlow and Holymire farms, though these are not rights of way. From Castle Nook to Thornhopeburn Bridge the Maiden Way coincides closely with the Pennine Way, and so can be followed without difficulty.)

Chapter Eight

From Thornhopeburn Bridge to Burnstones

AFTER CROSSING the Thornhope Burn the Maiden Way continues on its north-westerly course for another mile, as far as Slaggyford (the Pennine Way moves away east and follows a route nearer to the river). Immediately north of the crossing a collapsed stile stands on the Roman line, and in Bainbridge's time a solitary tree marked it in the middle of the first field north of the Burn. A single oak tree does in fact stand in the field but it hardly looks old enough to be the one referred to. There is no further visible sign of the road either in this field or in the next field to the north. However, as the Maiden Way approaches Thompson's Well Bridge it passes close by a large rock on a hilltop, and then as it descends the hill the ridge becomes evident, with signs of a ditch on its east side.

Just at the point where the side road to Thompson's Well Bridge leads off to the east, the A689 comes on to the line of the Maiden Way and follows it closely for the next mile or so to Slaggyford. Immediately south of the point where the roads coincide, on the eastern edge of the A689, a pavement of very large stones can be seen on the line of the Maiden Way. This may of course belong to a subsequent route following the line of the Maiden Way, but its appearance at this point is worthy of mention.

Hereabouts the reader – and more especially the walker – will have noticed how near the Roman road is to the South Tyne throughout this stretch; indeed for almost a mile north of Thompson's Well Bridge the river is very close indeed. This is rather unusual; Roman engineers, when following the course of a river, usually built their roads fairly high up on the valley side. In this case there were evidently problems in carrying the line further to the west; indeed the closeness of the A689 to the South Tyne in this area indicates that more recent road planners encountered the same difficulties.

At Slaggyford the Maiden Way alters its course to due north in step with the bend in the river. This brings it a little to the east of the A689 and almost parallel to it. In the field just north of the village a prominent ridge runs from south to north along the first rise of land from the flood plain and about 30 to 40 yards east of the main road, but further north there is little trace.

Just beyond Knarburn Cottage the Maiden Way and the A689

Ridge appears prominently both
north and south of this minor road

Knarsdale

Railway

A689

Slaggyford

Thompson's Well Bridge

South Tyne

Thornhopeburn Bridge

N

A view from the A689 of the ridge which runs north/south
to the east of it in the first field north of Slaggyford. The
trees mark the South Tyne.

Metalling on the line of the Maiden Way just where it joins
the A689 at Thompson's Well Bridge. The line of stones on
the right looks like a kerb.

The Maiden Way from
Thornhopeburn Bridge to Burnstones

again coincide for a short distance, but then the A689 swings north-east and the Roman road takes a more north-westerly direction which takes it away from the modern road. This occurs about a quarter of a mile north of Knarburn Cottage, and for the first 200 yards the line of the Maiden Way is marked by a farm track, which then swings off west to Sanders Close. The Maiden Way continues on its north-westerly course, and to meet it again we should continue north along the A689 to just beyond Knarsdale. Here a minor road runs off to the west (heading eventually for The Barns and Hanging Shaw). About 170 yards along this road a stile on the south side of the road marks the line of the Roman road, and the ridge appears very prominently crossing the field beyond.

In the field north of this minor road the ridge continues to be visible, and in the distance we see the line continued as a track climbing the high ground beyond Burnstones. This is actually the Pennine Way but, as we shall see, the two routes are close together for the next few miles.

(Note on access. Traces south of Thompson's Well Bridge may be seen from a track [with right of way] leading south from the A689 at this point – where also the pavement of large stones mentioned in the text may be studied. Just north of Slaggyford the ridge is quite visible from the main road [on its eastern side]; further north the detour along the side road to The Barns and Hanging Shaw is well worth while to see the ridge crossing it.)

The Maiden Way just south of the A689; note the substantial metalling in the foreground.

Nearly half a mile south of the A689; well-constructed culvert on the Maiden Way, which at this point is a green trackway.

Final descent to the north bank of Glendue (looking north); substantial ridge between ditches.

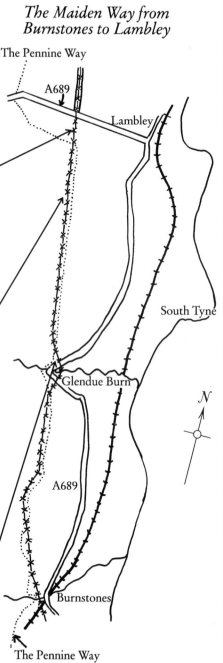

The Maiden Way from Burnstones to Lambley

The Pennine Way

A689

Lambley

South Tyne

Glendue Burn

A689

N

Burnstones

The Pennine Way

Chapter Nine

Burnstones to Lambley

AFTER CROSSING the Thinhope Burn at Burnstones, the Maiden Way is followed very closely by the Pennine Way until just south of the point where the A689 is crossed near Lambley – a distance of about three miles. For the first half mile or so, the Roman road is generally a little to the east of the Pennine Way, but it is so indistinct that the best plan is probably to follow the Pennine Way from the start, i.e. from the track that leads off between Burnstone House and the adjacent barn, heading north. After perhaps a third of a mile a disused quarry interrupts the route; it is easy to lose one's direction at this point. The Pennine Way and the Maiden Way head straight across the quarry to resume their line on the northern edge, and shortly afterwards they coincide and stay together thereafter.

The Maiden Way in this area is a wide grassy strip, quite raised in places, and with stone outcroppings at intervals. Further on it becomes a stony track, accompanied by a wall for some distance. The Glendue valley now comes into view, and the Maiden Way can be seen slanting up the opposite (northern) side of the valley from the east as a lighter strip before rejoining the main northern alignment. Evidently the Maiden Way must have been diverted to the east on the southern side also of Glendue, and actually a farm track does go off in that direction as the valley is approached. The actual crossing point is now masked by trees, but it must have been quite a distance east of the crossing point of the Pennine Way – which slopes in the opposite direction, to the west, on both banks of the Glendue Burn. In fact, the Roman crossing point was probably located east of the bridge which carries the A689 over the burn.

On the north side of Glendue, the ridge of the Maiden Way is seen in great strength, with side-ditches clearly marked, slanting up from the east to rejoin the main alignment some way up the hill. The Roman road is then followed by a wall or fence on its western side. For a long distance as it heads almost due north; the ridge continues to be evident. The road in this area shows very typical Roman characteristics – pronounced ridge in the vicinity of a stream crossing, together with local alteration of course to gain a good crossing place. The road metalling now starts to appear underfoot, especially where the surface is water-worn, and at one point the road passes over a well-constructed culvert. The view to the north starts to open up with the Maiden Way marked far ahead by a minor road, and, away in the distance, Walltown Crags looming up on the horizon to remind us that we are nearing Hadrian's Wall. Shortly before reaching the A689 the Pennine Way goes off to the west, climbing the fence by a high stile, but the Maiden Way continues straight ahead, slightly west of north, crosses the A689 at right angles just west of a conspicuous white building, and is then joined by a minor road which marks its line quite closely for the next two miles. Before leaving this section it is worth recording that from Glendue northwards the course we have followed is accompanied by a parish boundary; the Roman road enthusiast will recognise the significance of this.

(Note on access. There is of course no problem in this section, since the Maiden Way and the Pennine Way either coincide or are very close, so a right of way accompanies the route throughout.)

Looking north along the Maiden Way about 400 yards south of the point where it crosses the A689 west of Lambley. In the foreground the Roman road appears as a green track; the buildings mark the A689, and beyond this the line is taken up by a narrow minor road.

Chapter Ten

From Lambley to Carvoran
(*Magnis*)

Aᶠᵗᵉʳ ᶜʳᵒˢˢⁱⁿᵍ the A689, the minor road to Burnfoot and Peat Gate continues the line of the Maiden Way on the same alignment – almost due north. For the first mile or so, it would seem to follow the same line exactly, being very direct, and marked, for quite a distance by the parish boundary which has accompanied the course from Glendue. It is a narrow road and steep in parts, and as it approaches Hartley Burn it commences to wind. According to Bainbridge, these bends take it away from the line of the Roman road, which continues in the same straight line, although not now showing evident signs on the ground. However, after climbing Craig's bank, the straight Roman line is again joined, and two houses, called respectively Maidenway Cottage, and Maidenway House, stand alongside the road.

Shortly afterwards, we arrive at the deep gorge of Glen Cune, and at this point the Maiden Way leaves the modern road (which goes east and west at a T junction) and continues on its northwards course across Featherstone Common. In this rather remote spot, we can pause to study the Roman road as it climbs the steep north-east bank (north of the modern road bridge) after crossing the burn. It appears first as quite a prominent ridge, then as a damaged terrace, finally, at the top of the slope, as a very broad ridge with traces of the side-ditches. Going northward this ridge continues strong for some distance as it traverses the rough pasture. It is intermittently visible for the next half mile, after which it crosses, at right angles, the stream called Pinkins Cleugh. Looking back southward along the line from this point, one can plainly see the white building marking the point where the Maiden Way crosses the A689, and beyond that the line of the Roman road descending the hill.

The line now becomes more difficult to trace, but can be picked up again in about half a mile. The location is hard to describe but worth looking for. A short distance to the east of the Maiden Way is a minor road, also heading north (from Featherstone Bridge to Blekinsopp Castle). If we follow this road northwards we arrive at a small wood on its western side, clearly marked on the Pathfinder map (No. 546), just beyond the point where the road turns more to the north. The Maiden Way crosses the small stream at the western end of this wood – quite near the road – and it is clearly seen crossing

43

N

Magnis
(Roman fort)

Greenhead

B6318

Tipalt Burn

A69

On the higher ground at the top of the bank the road
appears as a broad ridge between ditches.

Featherstone
Common

Glen Cune

Looking south along the damaged terrace which carries the
Maiden Way up the steep bank of Glen Cune; the modern
bridge is just visible in the background.

A689
Lambley

*Final stretch of the Maiden Way;
the approach to the fort of* Magnis

the field south of the stream as a broad ridge. Incidentally, the stream is still forded, by a farm track, at precisely the point where the Maiden Way crosses it, and there is a great deal of stone in the stream bed at this point. In the field to the north of the stream the Roman road is still traceable as a very slight ridge, making a hump in the wall to the north.

Just over half a mile to the north, the minor road from Featherstone Bridge to Blekinsopp Castle bends to the west at the crossing of Wydon Cleugh. At the beginning of the bend a track leads off south-westwards, and a few yards along this track a tell-tale hump appears at the point where the Maiden Way crosses on its way northwards.

We are now only a mile from the terminus of the Maiden Way at the fort of Carvoran (MAGNIS), but though the course of the road has been established across the Tipalt Burn and beyond, its traces are so difficult to discern that this seems an appropriate point to conclude our survey. At MAGNIS the Maiden Way met the Stanegate, the road which we will visit next, and we shall be passing the point of intersection in the course of our exploration.

(Note on access. As far as Glen Cune, the by-road on or near the Maiden Way is narrow and often steep, but driveable with care. Featherstone Common is rough open pasture, though there is no right of way. However, the traces just north of Glen Cune Bridge – the most interesting in the area – can be studied, and access to intermittent traces further north is not difficult. The last mile to the fort of MAGNIS *runs over enclosed land, but near the crossing of the Tipalt Burn the line is crossed by a right of way and might repay investigation.)*

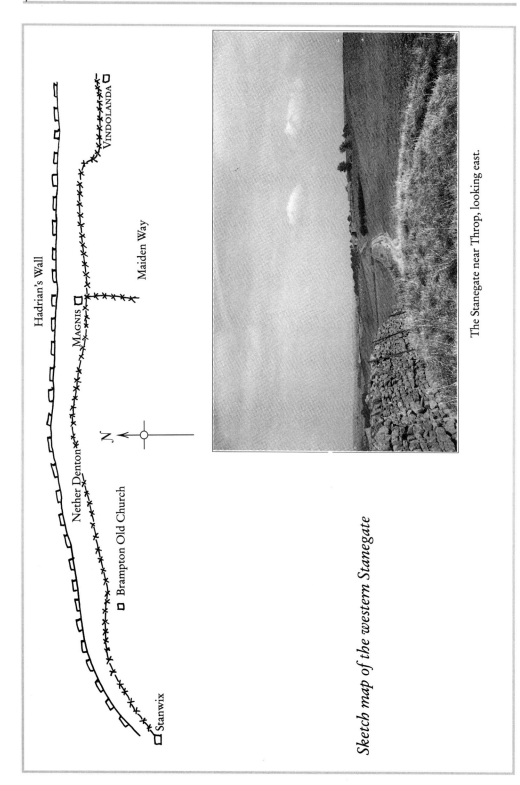

The Stanegate near Throp, looking east.

Sketch map of the western Stanegate

Within the map:

Hadrian's Wall

VINDOLANDA

MAGNIS

Maiden Way

Nether Denton

Brampton Old Church

Stanwix

N

Part Two

The Stanegate

Chapter One

General

WE DO NOT KNOW the Roman name of any single road in this country, but as was observed earlier, many of the principal ones were subsequently given names by the Anglo-Saxons. In the case of the Stanegate, the etymology is fairly simple. The second element of the name is derived from the old Norse 'gata', a road, so that the whole word means 'stony road', a reference to the metalling which distinguished this and the other Roman roads from the un-made tracks used by our early forebears.

This book is concerned only with the western section of the Stanegate, between VINDOLANDA and Carlisle, a distance of about 27 miles. Throughout this section the Stanegate runs from east to west, roughly parallel to Hadrian's Wall and not far south of it – generally within a mile and sometimes much closer. It links a number of forts along its route – for example, VINDOLANDA, Carvoran, Nether Denton, Brampton Old Church, and (probably) Stanwix in Carlisle. It is, in fact, a strongly fortified road. From this it has been argued that the Stanegate was an early frontier, predating the building of Hadrian's Wall; and while there are difficulties in accepting this for the entire road, it seems a plausible enough explanation for the section we are investigating.

The western Stanegate offers many points of interest, chief among them perhaps being the series of cuttings whereby it negotiates areas of difficulty in the country south of the River Irthing. The frequent recurrence of this feature is unparalleled in any other Roman road in Britain, so we shall devote a good deal of attention to it, without of course ignoring the other characteristics of this very interesting road.

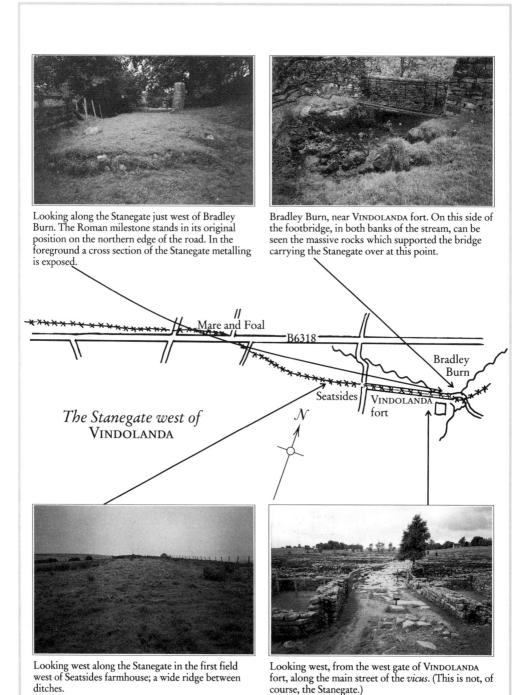

Looking along the Stanegate just west of Bradley Burn. The Roman milestone stands in its original position on the northern edge of the road. In the foreground a cross section of the Stanegate metalling is exposed.

Bradley Burn, near VINDOLANDA fort. On this side of the footbridge, in both banks of the stream, can be seen the massive rocks which supported the bridge carrying the Stanegate over at this point.

Mare and Foal

B6318

Bradley Burn

Seatsides

VINDOLANDA fort

The Stanegate west of VINDOLANDA

N

Looking west along the Stanegate in the first field west of Seatsides farmhouse; a wide ridge between ditches.

Looking west, from the west gate of VINDOLANDA fort, along the main street of the *vicus*. (This is not, of course, the Stanegate.)

Chapter Two

Vindolanda to Fell End Farm

VINDOLANDA is an ideal departure point for our exploration of the western Stanegate – a fine Roman fort with many interesting remains and a fascinating museum. The enthusiast will want to spend an hour or two here before setting off. The Stanegate does not pass through the fort itself, but runs from east to west just to the north; to find it we retrace our steps to the (visitors') entrance to the fort complex, and turn eastwards – away from the car park – along the track which passes the fort on its northern side, and which lies a little to the north of the actual course of the Stanegate. Our track crosses the Brackies Burn, and shortly afterwards arrives at the Bradley Burn, which it crosses by a footbridge. At this point the modern track has swung southward, across the Stanegate, and just to the north of the footbridge we see in both banks of the Bradley Burn the large stones which formed the supports of the Roman bridge by which the Stanegate crossed. More interesting still, a short distance to the west of the stream, on the northern edge of the Stanegate, stands a fine cylindrical Roman milestone. It is uninscribed, but still stands proudly in its original position, and provides us with a very suitable starting point for our westward journey along the Roman road.

The first stretch westwards is marked by the mile-long approach road to the car park and fort. This is now very narrow – so much so that passing places have to be provided for cars. One notices how-ever the wide grassy verges, indicating that the modern road occupies only a part of the width of the ridge on which the Stanegate was constructed, and which is still quite evident, rising to a height of some two or three feet. A narrow modern road or track following a broader ridge – with wide verges in consequence – is a frequent indication of a Roman line, as the seasoned follower will already know. Another and better known characteristic, also featured here, is the notable straightness of the alignments. However, as we shall see, the Stanegate in particular does not always follow this rule, especially when it gets into difficult country further west.

Not long before reaching the T junction which marks the western end of this minor road, the base of another Roman milestone is encountered, again in its original position. It is set back some dis-tance from the north edge of the present metalled surface, confirming our original observation that the original Stanegate was wider. Its distance from the milestone north of the fort is just under one mile;

the Roman mile was a little shorter than the present-day one – about eighty yards shorter, in fact. The incidence of two successive milestones makes one wonder whether the more important Roman roads had complete sets of milestones; if so, most of them have disappeared, for the number surviving in this country is around one hundred.

Shortly after this second milestone is passed we arrive at a T-junction, where our route is crossed by another minor road. Here the metalled section of the Stanegate ceases and a farm track – the approach to Seatsides Farm – takes up the line and follows it for about 200 yards. The track then swerves off to the south; the Stanegate, however, goes straight on over some rough ground, and the farmhouse appears to be built partly over it. The Roman road continues to be marked by a ridge in the fields to the west of the house, with traces of the ditches here and there. For about a third of a mile the line is roughly followed also by field walls just to the north of it.

The Stanegate now changes course more to the north, approaching nearer to the B6318 – the military road constructed by General Wade after the 1745 rebellion. Curiously enough this military road, built 1500 years after the Roman era, displays many of the characteristics one associates with Roman roads, since it was constructed for very much the same purpose. About a mile and a half west of Seatsides, the Stanegate crosses, almost at right angles, a minor road leading south (to Melkridge) from the B6813. At the crossing point, perhaps 150 yards south of the B6813, the ridge makes a hump in the Melkridge road and in the walls on either side. The Stanegate continues to be visible in the field to the west of the Melkridge Road, traversing this field diagonally in a north-westerly direction. It then slants across the B6813, almost at the point where a minor road leads off in the direction of Hadrian's Wall, and enters the field called the Mare and Foal, from two standing stones to the north of the Roman line. From the south-eastern corner of this field it is well seen as it slants up the hill in a direction just north of west.

The Stanegate now alters its line to south of west and for the next four miles follows a course about three hundred yards north of the (modern) military road (B6318) and roughly parallel to it. It is at times very evident, but can sometimes be difficult to distinguish from the numerous remains of Roman camps (many of them serving the troops who built the Wall) which characterise this area. In the field south of Markham Cottage the ridge, with side ditches, appears strongly; further west it is very clear indeed in the field to the north of Greenwood Farm, especially where it crosses the west wall of this field. About three quarters of a mile further on, just east of the Fell End Farm, the Stanegate again alters its course to slightly north of west and, curiously enough, the military road to the south makes the same change so that the two lines continue almost parallel.. The approach to the major fort of Carvoran (MAGNIS), which now commences, will be taken up in the next chapter.

(Notes on access. The remains north of VINDOLANDA *and the first mile westwards are of course fully accessible. The farm track to Seatsides [not a right of way] follows the line; west of the farm two tracks from the B6318, both with right of way, cross the Stanegate, which is then seen from the Melkridge Road, and the crossroads beyond, by the Mare and Foal field. West of this the line continues to be crossed by minor roads and rights of way.)*

Looking eastwards along the Stanegate from a point nearly one mile west of VINDOLANDA*. The Roman line is here followed by the modern approach road to the fort. Note the base of the Roman milestone on the left (north) edge of the road, marking the first Roman mile from* VINDOLANDA *– also the wide verge, typical of a more recent road following a Roman line.*

Looking west along the Stanegate in the third field west of Throp Farm. A bold ridge, banked steeply on the northern side, alongside a field wall.

Looking west along the Stanegate soon after it has crossed the Pennine Way west of Greenhead Golf Course; the road is more evident on the ground than in this picture.

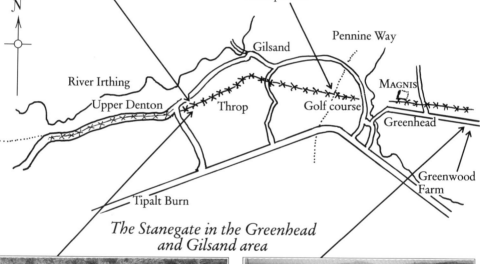

N

River Irthing

Upper Denton

Gilsand

Throp

Pennine Way

Golf course

MAGNIS

Greenhead

Greenwood Farm

Tipalt Burn

The Stanegate in the Greenhead and Gilsand area

Stone outcropping in the embanked northern side of the Stanegate in the third field west of Throp Farm.

North of Greenwood Farm—the ridge of the Stanegate is very clear indeed.

Chapter Three

Fell End Farm – Carvoran – Chapelburn

As THE FORT of Carvoran (which the Romans called MAGNIS) is approached, the Stanegate continues to be evident parallel to the B6318 and about 200/300 yards north of it. It crosses the field west of Fell End Farm buildings as a well-marked grassy ridge, and between this field and the next field to the west the metalling shows clearly in the ditch which intervenes. The ridge continues prominent right up to the minor road which crosses the Stanegate at right angles about 300 yards east of the remains of the fort. From here almost to the site of the east wall of the fort a field wall marks the line. Of the fort itself little is now visible – though many remains and much information can be studied at the nearby Roman museum. Likewise there is nothing now visible of the meeting point of the Stanegate with the Maiden Way, which seems to have been located at or near the south-east corner of the fort.

Shortly after leaving the fort the course of the Stanegate becomes obscure as it enters the valley of the Tipalt Burn. On the other side of the burn, however, we meet it again on Greenhead Golf Course, slanting up from the south and then resuming the same alignment as it followed on the eastern side of the valley. Also very prominent indeed across the golf course is the *Vallum* – the deep ditch, with flanking mounds, which runs just south of Hadrian's Wall, and parallel to it, throughout its length. The *Vallum* is spectacular in this area, and rather dwarfs the Stanegate, which is seen as a ridge of rough grass gradually slanting towards the *Vallum* and then following a course parallel to it and perhaps 100 yards to the south.

At the wall which forms the western boundary of the golf course, the Stanegate crosses, at right angles, the Pennine Way, and the *Vallum* continues its impressive course just to the north. In the western half of this rough field (the first beyond the golf course) the Stanegate is also prominent, a bold ridge running for over 100 yards right up to the western field wall, with the side ditches clearly showing. The next field to the west has evidently been cultivated, for the *Vallum* itself has almost been ploughed out, while the Roman road appears very faintly, running towards a very small triangular wood in the angle between two field walls (marked, though not too obviously, on the O.S. Pathfinder map [No. 546]).

Further west, south-west of Chapel House, the ridge is plainly seen, fading however as the minor road leading to The Gap is approached. Once again the *Vallum* is very evident, crossing the two fields to the north in great strength.

South of Gilsand the Stanegate swings south, away from the *Vallum*, and takes up a south-westerly course, which in half a mile falls into the eastern approach track to Throp farm, which follows the Roman line for about 200 yards. When the path slants off to the south, the Stanegate carries straight ahead to pass the northern edge of the farm buildings, after which the track leading westwards away from Throp coincides with it.

Now commences a very interesting section of the Stanegate; for more than half a mile it runs, quite straight, as a terraceway, steeply embanked on its northern side. Quite often the stones building up this bank are visible. The track which accompanies the line across the first field west of the farmhouse then swings north to the (modern) road; the terraceway continues but is masked in the second field by the wall built immediately to the north of it. However, the embankment is again well seen in the third field, often four or five feet high with frequent outcrops of retaining stone.

This fine stretch comes to an end when the line of the Stanegate is taken up by the minor road to Chapelburn, just after this has branched off the road from Gilsand. For nearly two miles to Chapelburn this road follows a fairly direct course (though far from straight in detail – it was diverted for the railway crossing west of Upper Denton) and it probably roughly represents the course of the Stanegate. Just beyond Chapelburn the Roman fort at Nether Denton is passed and the same road, continuing to Low Row, probably continues to follow the approximate course of the Stanegate for some

The embanked Stanegate just under half a mile west of Throp farm, looking west.

distance; certainly the village name, Beckstonegate, about a mile further on, seems to suggest this.

(Note on access. The approach to MAGNIS *from the east is near the B6318 and crossed by a right of way at Fell End and a minor road just east of the fort. Across Greenhead Golf Course a right of way follows the* Vallum, *just to the north of the Stanegate, and further west, in the interesting area around Throp, tracks follow the line, though they are not marked as rights of way on the O.S. maps.)*

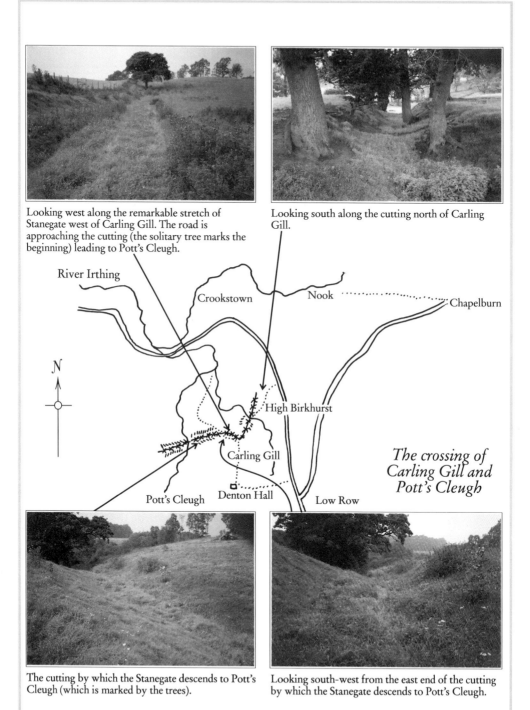

Looking west along the remarkable stretch of Stanegate west of Carling Gill. The road is approaching the cutting (the solitary tree marks the beginning) leading to Pott's Cleugh.

Looking south along the cutting north of Carling Gill.

River Irthing

Crookstown

Nook

Chapelburn

N

High Birkhurst

Carling Gill

The crossing of Carling Gill and Pott's Cleugh

Pott's Cleugh   Denton Hall   Low Row

The cutting by which the Stanegate descends to Pott's Cleugh (which is marked by the trees).

Looking south-west from the east end of the cutting by which the Stanegate descends to Pott's Cleugh.

Chapter Four

The Crossing of Carling Gill and Pott's Cleugh

AFTER LEAVING the rather uncertain section of the Stanegate beyond Chapelburn, we lose the line altogether, for the course has not been established for the next mile or so. Indeed the road is now entering very difficult country – south of the River Irthing – in which definite traces are lacking for considerable distances. From Chapelburn to Irthington – about six miles as the crow flies – the Stanegate is recognisable only at a few scattered points. However, the stretches that are known in this area are probably the most interesting in the whole route; to some extent, at any rate, they are unique in Roman Britain. They occur in the first instance where the road has had to traverse quite steep valleys running up to the Irthing from the south. This has been done by excavating deep cuttings – remarkable feats of engineering which remain well preserved. The same technique has been used, as we shall see, to overcome less obvious obstacles further west along the route.

The first example occurs about a mile west of Nook, where two streams, Carling Gill and Pott's Cleugh, flow northwards to the Irthing. The streams are quite close to each other, and the banks of Pott's Cleugh are densely wooded. Carling Gill is the first stream encountered as one approaches from the east, and a track, leading ultimately to Denton Hall, crosses the gill by means of a ford. Just west of this track, near the ford, a cutting has been made through the north bank of the gill (which flows almost east to west at this point). The cutting is about thirty yards long and perhaps fifteen to twenty feet wide; it runs almost due north-south and points directly to the ford. It is not a recent work, as the size of the trees growing in it indicate; indeed its resemblance to other cuttings encountered further west along the Stanegate points conclusively to a Roman origin. There is a good deal of stone in the floor of the cutting; and though there has been some collapse of the walls – the local rock is a soft red sandstone – the general outline is well preserved. The fact that the cutting points directly to the ford indicates that this also was in use in Roman times.

Across the ford the Roman road is clearly visible, going first south and then swinging west, following the contours of the land to secure a level course. It is accompanied right to the edge of Pott's Cleugh by field boundaries and for some of the way (conveniently) by a right of way. It appears to run through a much shallower cutting, within which the road itself is quite raised, especially after turning in a westerly direction. The ditches are marked by a denser growth of vegetation and metalling appears in the surface with distinct signs of a kerb on the northern edge in places. All in all a most interesting and well-preserved section.

As Pott's Cleugh is approached another cutting commences, on a larger scale than anything so far encountered. This was thoroughly examined in 1935 (Simpson and others, 1936), when it was found to be about 150 yards long. It deepens gradually as it approaches the wooded banks of the cleugh, reaching a maximum depth of at least twenty feet. A similar cutting leads westwards out of the cleugh, but nowadays this is much more difficult to approach and investigate. Metalling was found in both cuttings, and there seems no doubt of their Roman origin.

For the next mile or so to the west, no remains of the Stanegate have yet been recorded. This is not to say they do not exist; a road constructed on such a scale must have left traces even in the most unpromising terrain, and in all probability they will eventually be identified.

(Note on access. The path west of High Birkhurst Farm – leading to Denton Hall – gives access to the ford across Carling Gill; though not marked as right of way it appears to continue a path that is so marked. As mentioned above, much of the course of the Stanegate between Carling Gill and Pott's Cleugh is followed by another right of way, though this is difficult to find except by way of the path to Denton Hall.)

Chapter Five

Quarry Beck

ABOUT A MILE and a half west of Pott's Cleugh, the Stanegate has
another formidable obstacle to negotiate in the stream called
Quarry Beck, and here again the engineers have left impressive
remains. This particular stretch is best approached from the western
side and followed from west to east because in this way access is
much easier.

The best approach is along the lane which leads south-east from
the Brampton–Lanercost Road just east of Boothby. The lane, which
leads to the sawmill standing on Quarry Beck, is deeply sunken and
is in fact very near (just to the east of) the curving line of the cutting
whereby the Stanegate descended this very steep and deep ravine.

Quarry Beck is crossed at the end of the lane, on the sawmill site,
and the line of the Stanegate is more easily studied on the other –
south-eastern – side of the stream. Here the Stanegate ascends from
the ravine in an impressive cutting, running south-eastwards, which
clearly originated from a natural gully, deepened and widened. The
gully – and cutting – bend more to the south as the hill is climbed;
this probably originated as a natural curve but has been converted,
in true Roman style, into a succession of straight lines. A fence
follows the line throughout. In places the bottom of the cutting
shows distinct signs of having been levelled and widened to accom-
modate the road, and every so often the metalling outcrops. Occasionally a build-up of stones is visible, shoring up the sides of the
cutting.

Trial holes in the 1935 investigation (Simpson and others, 1936),
revealed metalling in the floor of the cutting, together with a series
of wooden stakes which probably served to strengthen the sides. The
length of the work is about 100 yards, after which the eastward
course of the Stanegate becomes uncertain. However the line is then
crossed by a lane, heading in an easterly direction towards Naworth
Castle, and where this meets the minor road, south of the castle, the
road bends significantly to follow an east-west line for some distance. This is, of course, no more than an indication of a possible
route.

Likewise there is no firm evidence for the course of the Stanegate
to the west of its approach to Quarry Beck, though here again the
relatively straight stretch of road/lane/footpath by Boothby Cottages and onwards, passing north of Brampton, might provide a
pointer.

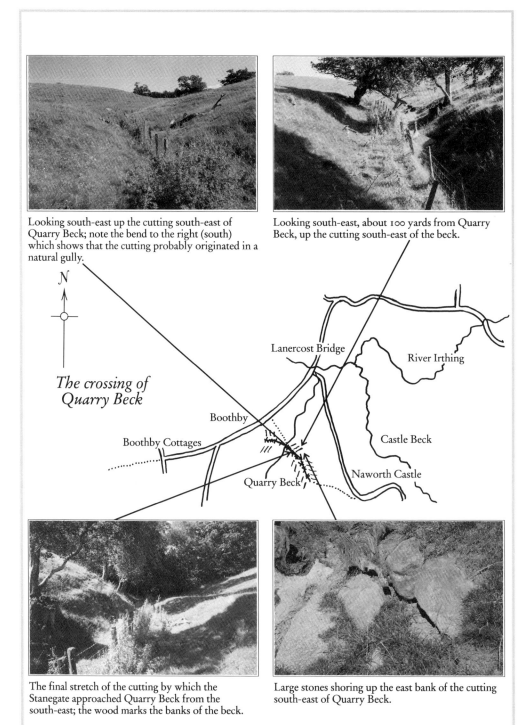

Looking south-east up the cutting south-east of Quarry Beck; note the bend to the right (south) which shows that the cutting probably originated in a natural gully.

Looking south-east, about 100 yards from Quarry Beck, up the cutting south-east of the beck.

The crossing of Quarry Beck

N

Lanercost Bridge

River Irthing

Boothby

Castle Beck

Boothby Cottages

Naworth Castle

Quarry Beck

The final stretch of the cutting by which the Stanegate approached Quarry Beck from the south-east; the wood marks the banks of the beck.

Large stones shoring up the east bank of the cutting south-east of Quarry Beck.

(Note on access. The lane to the sawmill gives access to the crossing point of the beck, but there should be no difficulty in securing permission – and directions – to study the Roman cutting on the other side.)

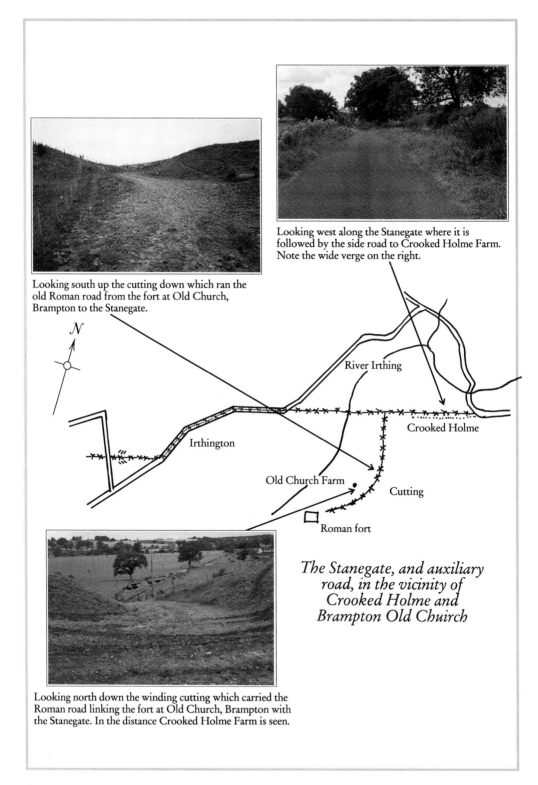

Looking south up the cutting down which ran the old Roman road from the fort at Old Church, Brampton to the Stanegate.

Looking west along the Stanegate where it is followed by the side road to Crooked Holme Farm. Note the wide verge on the right.

N

River Irthing

Irthington

Crooked Holme

Old Church Farm

Cutting

Roman fort

The Stanegate, and auxiliary road, in the vicinity of Crooked Holme and Brampton Old Chuirch

Looking north down the winding cutting which carried the Roman road linking the fort at Old Church, Brampton with the Stanegate. In the distance Crooked Holme Farm is seen.

Chapter Six

Crooked Holme and Brampton Old Church

A S INDICATED at the end of the last chapter, the series of footpaths and lanes continuing the line of the side road past Boothby Cottages may give some indication of the direction of the Stanegate in the area north of Brampton; if so, it must then have altered course more to the north thereafter – not unlikely in this difficult terrain. The next undoubted section to the west is to be found in the lane approaching Crooked Holme Farm, just east of the Irthing, together with the short stretch of the A6071 which precedes it. The lane and main road together make up a straight stretch of nearly half a mile, and at the farm a field boundary continues the line to the River Irthing.

The lane from the main road to Crooked Holme gives indications of following an engineered route, not one that has simply grown up for convenience of approach. For part of its length it runs through quite a wide cutting; elsewhere it is an embanked causeway as it crosses two shallow depressions. Occasionally it has wide verges, invariably a sign of an old road, and the sharp bends which bring the A6071 on and off the line are common indications of the influence of a Roman road.

In previous chapters we have noted the occurrence of forts along the Stanegate (VINDOLANDA, MAGNIS) without dwelling on them, since this is not our purpose – other forts, indeed, we have left unmentioned. But at Crooked Holme the Stanegate passes a fort (Roman name unknown) which is linked to the Stanegate by a branch road which merits notice.

The fort in question is situated high on a bluff overlooking the river, nearly half a mile south of Crooked Holme and immediately south-west of Old Church Farm. The site is now occupied by part of a large cemetery – the old Brampton graveyard – in the midst of which stands a small chapel. Hence the name 'The Old Church Fort'. The road linking the fort with the Stanegate descends on a curving course – first eastwards and then northwards through a deep cutting which closely resembles the examples encountered in previous chapters. For some of its length the present farm road makes use of this cutting (joining it where it passes to the east of the farm buildings); whether the continuation of the farm road on lower ground continues the Roman line is doubtful, but it is certainly heading in the right direction – due north, and hence towards the Stanegate (Simpson and Richmond, 1936).

(Note on access. From the by-road to Crooked Holme a track, with right of way, gives access to the cutting described above and to the cemetery which now overlies the Roman fort.)

Another view northwards down the cutting which carried the Roman road from the fort at Brampton Old Church down to the Stanegate.

Chapter Seven

Buckjumping and Crosby Lodge

THE lane to Crooked Holme ends about a quarter of a mile east of the River Irthing, and a field boundary continues the line to the river. It seems then that the crossing was on this line; indeed remains of an ancient bridge have been discovered in the river hereabouts (St Joseph, 1935, in Simpson and others, 1936); hardly Roman but perhaps at or near the site of a Roman predecessor.

The course past Crooked Holme, continued across the river, falls into the main street of Irthington village at Gallowberry. This street follows a south-west course through the village, changing direction in short straight lengths. It very likely marks the course of the Roman road, keeping to the edge of the higher ground above the river flood plain, and bringing the road conveniently to the beginning of the next long alignment, commencing on the high point of Red Hills.

Here the Stanegate resumes the straight course interrupted in the difficult country south of the Irthing, and follows a line south of west which takes it to the outskirts of Carlisle. Almost immediately there occurs another of those cuttings which have been such a feature of the route, curious in this case, since there seems no adequate reason for the effort involved.

The site is a farm with the rather strange name of Buckjumping, just east of Red Hills. Here a small hill, in the middle of a field, stands directly in the path of the Roman road. The hill is visible from the two (modern) roads which skirt the field on its southern and eastern edges, but there is no track giving access, and permission should be sought for a closer inspection, which is well worthwhile. The road has been driven straight through the hill in a cutting about sixty yards long and twenty feet deep. Admittedly the rock is the soft red sandstone of the area, but the labour involved must have been considerable, and it would not have been difficult to circumvent the obstacle or even to go over it.

So unusual is this piece of road engineering that its Roman origin was in the past called into question. Excavation in 1896 showed a substantial road surface in the cutting at a depth of four feet, but this was presumed to be a sunken road of a more recent date. However, further research (Simpson and others, 1936) has established beyond doubt that this is Roman work – of the type already noted at Pott's Cleugh, Quarry Beck and Old Church. Among the supporting evidence is its position exactly on the long alignment commencing

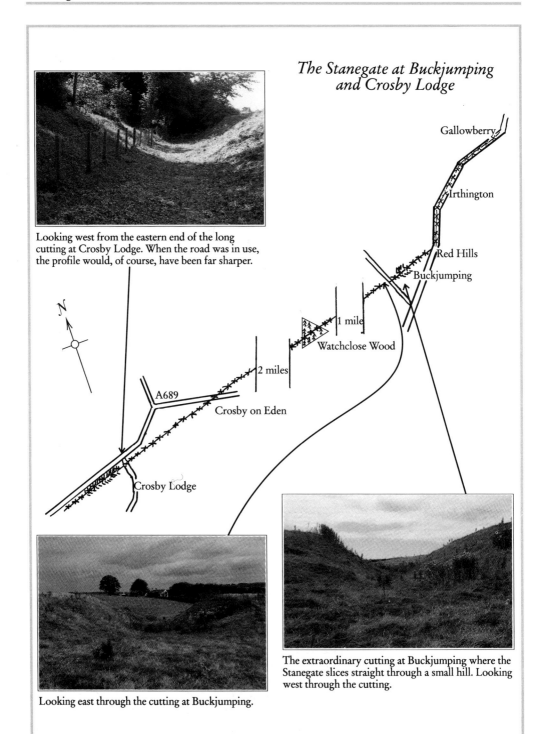

The Stanegate at Buckjumping and Crosby Lodge

Looking west from the eastern end of the long cutting at Crosby Lodge. When the road was in use, the profile would, of course, have been far sharper.

Gallowberry

Irthington

Red Hills

Buckjumping

1 mile

Watchclose Wood

2 miles

A689

Crosby on Eden

Crosby Lodge

Looking east through the cutting at Buckjumping.

The extraordinary cutting at Buckjumping where the Stanegate slices straight through a small hill. Looking west through the cutting.

at Red Hills and confirmed at several points to the west, even where not now apparent.

There is little trace of the Stanegate in the ground on each side of the cutting, and further investigation to the west is ruled out by the siting of Carlisle Airport, which stretches for the next mile or so. However, before the airport was constructed, the ridge was found well preserved in Watchclose Wood (where the ground had escaped the plough) and trenching confirmed the road at this point, exactly on a straight line between Buckjumping and our next point of investigation at High Crosby.

This lies about three miles south-west of Buckjumping and is the last of the Stanegate sites to be investigated in detail. Once again it is a spectacular piece of road construction; yet another cutting, the longest encountered on the whole route. To find it we must go westwards from Crosby-on-Eden along the A689 Brampton to Carlisle main road (shown as the B6264 on older maps). After about half a mile we come upon a turning to the left (south) and just afterwards, on the south side of the A689, a sign indicating the Crosby Lodge Hotel. This sign marks the eastern end of the cutting, which then runs alongside the A689 on its southern side and parallel to it.

The cutting is quite unmistakable, like a deep gully. On my last visit (1991) the first 30/40 yards had been cleared of vegetation, making it clearer still; the remainder is overgrown with trees and scrub, but very evident. The cutting is about 250 yards long, about thirty yards wide and some fifteen feet deep. It is exactly aligned with the cutting at Buckjumping and with the ridge in Watchclose Wood which intervenes (and with field boundaries marking the line west of the airport). The soft sandstone of the walls has tended to collapse; when first constructed the cutting must have been far sharper and the bottom more level.

Trial holes sunk in 1934/5 (Simpson and others, 1936) revealed substantial metalling continuing for the whole length of the floor of the cutting, with shallow gutters on each side of the metalling. Associated with the road were a few shards of Roman pottery, thus placing its origin beyond doubt. There seems even less reason here for such substantial rock cutting than at Buckjumping. It is nevertheless fortunate for future archaeologists that the Stanegate engineers were so ambitious, otherwise it would have been difficult indeed to establish the line of the road in east Cumbria.

At the western end of the cutting the course of the road once again becomes indeterminate, but it seems clear that it was heading for the fort of Stanwix in north Carlisle, near the River Eden. The A689 runs in straight lengths in the same direction, and probably represents, at least approximately, the course of the Stanegate for the remaining distance.

(Note on access. As noted above, there is no public access to the cutting at Buckjumping, and the reader must be content with studying it from the two adjacent roads, or should ask permission for a closer inspection. There is no such problem at High Crosby, for though some of the cutting lies just within the fence marking the boundary of the Crosby lodge grounds, it can nevertheless be thoroughly seen and inspected from the side of the main road.)

Epilogue

IT goes without saying that two such notable Roman roads as the Maiden Way and the Stanegate have attracted the attention of archaeologists through the years, and it might be of interest to conclude with a brief account of the studies which have been made, and especially of the excavation which has taken place from time to time.

We have frequently referred to the survey of the Maiden Way made by William Bainbridge. Writing in 1855, he was early in the field. Indeed his investigation came soon after the great enclosure movement of the late eighteenth and early nineteenth centuries, when common land was being divided up and cultivated. Again and again, in his survey, he remarked how the metalling of the Roman road had recently been removed, either to provide stone for the new field walls or to clear the way for the plough. A typical example is that of Featherstone Common, the tract of country still so marked on the O.S. Pathfinder map (No. 546) north of Glencune. Bainbridge notes that the 'Featherstone Common Inclosure Act' had been passed in 1808, and by the time he wrote, much of the stone from the stretch of Maiden Way crossing the common was either built into the new walls or had been heaped up at the edge of the fields. It is evident that this was a time of great destruction of Roman roads. For all that, Bainbridge gives the impression that in his day far more was visible of this remarkable road than is to be seen to-day.

Not very much recorded excavation seems to have taken place along the Maiden Way. In this respect, the Stanegate has been better served. This is partly due to the series of remarkable cuttings which occur in its western potion and which have been described above; excavation has been needed to establish that these cuttings do indeed represent the course of the Roman road. But another reason is furnished by the considerable number of occupation sites – forts, etc. – which occur along the Stanegate; the road has inevitably been studied in connection with these.

Thus in the neighbourhood of VINDOLANDA several sections were dug across the road in 1935/6. It was found to be around eighteen to twenty feet wide, built up of sandstone blocks, with a high camber and bounding kerb (Wright, 1937). Earlier excavation further west, in the Denton area, gave much the same picture – a road about 18/19 feet wide with substantial metalling and with the kerb occasionally preserved (Simpson and others, 1913). A more recent investigation, in 1978, was concerned once again with the ravine by which the Stanegate approached Quarry Beck from the west – a natural ravine possibly adapted for the road, substantial remains of which were found (Richardson, 1978).

No doubt much remains to be discovered about these two re-markable roads, but not, perhaps, by excavation. Indeed at the end of the first systematic study of British Roman roads, by Thomas Codrington, in 1903, the following words are found (and they may stand as the conclusion of this little study) 'They are generally found under an accumulation of soil, and it would seem that their future preservation would be best secured by leaving them as much as possible under such a protective covering.'

The Maiden Way, look-ing north from south of the Glendue valley. Note how the road swerves to the east as it descends the opposite (northern) side.

Bibliography

Abbreviated forms in brackets.

(*Arch. Ael.* = *Archaeologia Aeliana*)

(Trans. C.&W.A.&A.S. = *Transactions of the Cumberland and Westmorland Antiquarian and Archaeological Society*)

Bainbridge W., 'Account of the Roman road called "The Maiden Way" ', *Arch. Ael.* IV, 36, (1855) (Bainbridge, 1855)

Collingwood R. G., 'Two Roman Mountain Roads', Trans. C.&W.A.&A.S., N.S. XXXVII, 1, (1937) (Collingwood, 1937)

Codrington T., *Roman Roads in Britain* (SPCK, 1918) (Codrington, 1918)

Gibbons P., with Bartlett A., Hird L., McCarthy M., Rackham J., Van der Veen M., Wild F., 'Excavations and Observations at Kirkby Thore', Trans. C.&W.A.&A.S., LXXXIX, 93, (1989) (Gibbons and others, 1989)

Higham N., and Jones B., *The Carvetii* (Alan Sutton, 1985) (Higham & Jones, 1985)

Margary I. D., *Roman Roads in Britain* (Phoenix, 1957) (Margary, 1957)

Ordnance Survey Map of Roman Britain (O.S., 1991)

Richardson G. G. S., 'A Section of the Stanegate at Boothby, Cumbria', Trans. C.&W.A.&A.S., N.S. LXXVIII, 206, (1978) (Richardson, 1978)

Simpson F. G., Richmond I. A., Hodgson K. S., St Joseph K., 'Report of the Cumberland Excavation Committee for 1935; §4, The Stanegate', Trans. C.&W.A.&A.S., N.S. XXXVI, 182, (1936) (Simpson and others, 1936)

Simpson F. G. and Richmond I. A., 'Report of the Cumberland Excavation Committee for 1935; §3, The Roman Fort on the Stanegate, and other remains, at Old Church, Brampton', Trans. C.&W.A.&A.S., N.S. XXXVI, 172, (1936) (Simpson and Richmond, 1936)

Simpson F. G., Haverfield F., Craster H.H.E., and Newbold P., 'Excavations on the Line of the Roman Wall in Cumberland during the Years 1909–12, Trans. C.&W.A.&A.S., N.S. XII, 297, (1913) (Simpson and others, 1913)

Wright R. P., 'The Stanegate at Chesterholm', *Arch. Ael.* XIV (4th Series), 185, (1937) (Wright, 1937)

Occasional Papers from the Centre for North-West Regional Studies

Flowering Plants and Ferns of Cumbria	G. Halliday	£2.95
Early Lancaster Friends	M. Mullet	£2.95
North-West Theses and Dissertations, 1950–78	U. Lawler	£6.00
Lancaster: The Evolution of its Townscape to 1800	S. Penney	£2.95
Richard Marsden and the Preston Chartists, 1837–48	J. King	£2.95
The Grand Theatre, Lancaster	A. Betjemann	£2.95
Popular Leisure and the Music Hall in 19th-century Bolton	R. Poole	£2.95
The Diary of William Fisher of Barrow, 1811–59	W. Rollinson/B. Harrison	£2.95
Rural Life in South-West Lancashire, 1840–1914	A. Mutch	£3.95
Grand Fashionable Nights: Kendal Theatre, 1575–1985	M. Eddershaw	£3.95
The Roman Fort and Town of Lancaster	D. Shotter/A. White	£4.95
Windermere in the nineteenth century	O. M. Westall	£4.95
A Traditional Grocer: T. D. Smith's of Lancaster	M. Winstanley	£4.95
Reginald Farrer: Dalesman, Planthunter, Gardener	J. Illingworth/J. Routh	£4.95
Walking Roman Roads in Bowland	P. Graystone	£4.95
The Royal Albert: Chronicles of an Era	J. Alston	£4.95
From Lancaster to the Lakes – The Region in Literature	K. Hanley/A. Milbank	£5.95
The Buildings of Georgian Lancaster	A. White	£5.95
Lydia Becker and The Cause	A. Kelly	£5.95
Romans and Britons in North-West England	D. Shotter	£5.95
S. Martin's College, Lancaster, 1964–89	P. Gedge/L. Louden	£5.95

Each of these titles may be ordered by post from:

C.N.W.R.S.,
Fylde College,
University of Lancaster,
Bailrigg, Lancaster

Books will be despatched post free to UK addresses.
Please make cheques payable to 'The University of Lancaster'.
Titles are also available from all good booksellers within the region.